Tangents

the truth can only be approached, if at all, obliquely, nor directly

but if one thinks of truth as a circle, the best one can hope for is to graze it momentarily to brush against, it or graze it momentarily

The human mind cannot seize truth in its full vital heart or essence

Essays and Reflections

Martin Henry

First published 2008 by
Veritas Publications
7/8 Lower Abbey Street
Dublin 1
Ireland
Email publications@veritas.ie
Website www.veritas.ie

ISBN 978 1 84730 063 8

Copyright © Martin Henry, 2008

10 9 8 7 6 5 4 3 2 1

Lines from Louis MacNeice's *Autumn Journal, A Poem* courtesy of Faber, 1943. Lines from Les Murray's 'The Knockdown Question' taken from *Poems the Size of Photographs,* courtesy of Duffy & Snellgrove, 2002. Lines from W.B. Yeats' 'Two Songs from a Play' taken from *Collected Poems*, courtesy of AP Watt Literary Agancy.

A catalogue record for this book is available from the British Library.
Cover design by Paula Ryan
Printed in the Republic of Ireland by Betaprint, Dublin
Veritas books are printed on paper made from the wood pulp of managed forests. For every tree felled, at least one tree is planted, thereby renewing natural resources.

In Memory of
Sean Javier Henry Cabrera
21 August 2002 – 27 June 2007

Contents

THE DOCTRINE OF CHRIST

THE KINGDOM OF HEAVEN

BETWEEN HEAVEN AND EARTH

RELIGION AND MORALITY

CHURCH MATTERS

CHRISTIANITY AND POWER

DEATH AND ETERNAL LIFE

ASPECTS OF THE HISTORY OF CHRISTIANITY

Preface

This is a collection of short essays and reflections on Christianity. Why *Tangents*? Simply because truth can, if at all, be approached only obliquely. Who could claim to have penetrated some inner circle of truth that might be considered its fundamental heart or essence? Perhaps, as human beings, the best we can hope for is to be able to brush against it, in the way that a tangent touches the circumference of a circle, before heading off again into the unknown.

In bringing together these reflections I hope that the various brushes with truth attempted here might stimulate some further thought on the great claims of the Christian faith that the church has handed down to us from the distant past. Its guiding spirit could be fairly summed up in the Latin adage, *'non nova, sed nove'*: 'not new things, but a new way of looking at things.' In other words, this book will succeed if it manages to illuminate, in some small way, the gift of what we have inherited.

This is, first and foremost, a book to be dipped into at random, a series of reflections designed in turn to encourage reflection, and this by looking at some fairly intractable issues that might be familiar, but from an angle that is perhaps less so. Its origin lies in the suggestion put to me that it would be useful to bring together different pieces that have been published in various places over the years. To this end I have made extensive use of homilies and short essays that have already appeared in print, and added some new material. For permission to use items already published, sometimes in a modified form, I am grateful to the editors and publishers of *The Furrow*, *Irish Theological Quarterly* (and SAGE Publications, London), *The Word*, *Doctrine and Life* and *The Irish Times*.

If, for the material of this work, I have chosen different subject areas, this is not in any way to suggest that a particular subject will be 'covered' in the book, but only to allow readers to make their way more easily around it. For this same reason, each element in the various sections has been given a specific title. Where a piece originated in a homily, I have indicated this in a footnote. I have also retained the original style of these various homilies, and added an index of them, for the benefit of readers who may wish to source a homily for a particular occasion.

I wish to record my thanks to Ronan Drury, D. Vincent Twomey, Michael A. Conway, Sarah Mac Donald, Bernard Treacy, Patsy McGarry, Caitriona Clarke and Ruth Kennedy of Veritas Publications, and John Campbell, who first prompted me to gather these reflections together in one volume.

Finally, I would like to dedicate this book to my little grand-nephew, Sean, whose tragic and untimely death earlier this year has left a permanent wound in the hearts of those who knew and loved him. *Toujours aimer, toujours souffrir, toujours mourir ...*[1]

Martin Henry
St Patrick's College
Maynooth
Co. Kildare

December 2007

THE QUESTION OF CREATION

GOD AND THE 'BIG BANG'

The term 'big bang,' referring to a primordial event believed to have initially sent the universe on its way, has now entered general cultural consciousness even in the case of those, like the present writer, who are innocent of the most rudimentary notions of natural science or astrophysics. It is permissible, however, for non-scientists to suggest that there might be, at first sight anyway, something odd in the fact that unrepentant non-transcendentalists appear to seek an explanation for the current state of the cosmos by trying to trace everything back to an origin. For can one have a 'belief' in an origin without a belief in an ultimate, transcendent 'originator' or 'creator'?

If the idea of a transcendent creator of the universe is abandoned, it would seem that the idea of an origin and an end, an 'alpha' and an 'omega' as it were, has to be abandoned also. In a world without any transcendent, divine sponsor, there can be no creation and no eschatology. Such a conclusion would seem to be inescapable. Hence whatever grand notions of origins or beginnings or ends or goals or purposes are still present in our culture would have to be viewed, presumably, as atavistic remnants of an archaic but now obsolete world view, somewhat like the appendix in the human body. Such remnants still exist simply because they have not yet been clearly recognised as no longer legitimately belonging to a world where there is no beginning or end, a world that is, to borrow Nietzsche's term, 'innocent' of any ultimate or transcendent significance. Indeed in any other than a workaday, pragmatic sense, concepts like 'origin' and 'end' are not conceivable at all. The thought of an absolute beginning or an absolute end would seem to be self-contradictory or at least self-defeating. How can one get behind an absolute beginning or beyond an absolute end in order to observe or conceive of them?

In describing the world process as 'the *innocence* of becoming' ('die *Unschuld* des Werdens[1]'), Nietzsche was drawing defiantly and exuberantly the (for him) only compelling, even if (for others) unpalatable, conclusion from his dismissal of any notion of divine transcendence. Unless, of course, one reckons that the very notion of an ultimate 'conclusion' is 'out of bounds' in a world without end (or beginning) and hence without meaning. Yet it is surely an irony that Christianity itself pins its own hopes on the prospect of divine bliss for all believers in a world, albeit beyond this world (*vita venturi saeculi*), but still a world without end, *per omnia saecula saeculorum*. The irony is compounded by the fact that Nietzsche, who wanted so desperately to purge himself of Christianity, may have succeeded only in transposing the substance of Christianity's own eschatology into a different, even if this-worldly, key.

ENVIRONMENT OR CREATION?[2]

The Christian doctrine of 'creation' acknowledges God to be the universe's unique, transcendent and abiding source. But in seeming to present God as an isolated absolute, a dominating force over the world, this doctrine has been interpreted as sowing in human beings, 'made in God's image', the seeds of an exploitative attitude towards the environment. Since the late-eighteenth century, in reaction to this misunderstanding, a newer, more 'immanentist' and almost pantheistic view of God's relationship to the world would prefer to see God as 'immanent' or present in the world, practically in the sense of being 'contained by' the world or being the world's spirit or soul.

This more recent view encourages Christians to live out their faith not in traditional flight from the world, but as life-affirmers, even as 'friends of the earth'. Yet the widespread increase in sensitivity to the environment prompts the question, 'Whose environment?' The answer, surely, must be, 'Humanity's environment'. But who, then, or what decrees humanity to be the centre of the universe around which, as the term 'environment' hints, everything else revolves? Humanity itself? Christianity, however, sees God, rather than humanity, as being centre stage.

If, nevertheless, the attempt were made to develop a fully-fledged, pantheistic, and thus 'immanentist' understanding of God in creation, this would not only mean a radical departure from the traditional Christian doctrine of creation, but it would also, more ominously, have implications for the doctrine of redemption. In a pantheistic or quasi-pantheistic perspective, 'redemption' could only mean either a blanket endorsement of everything that is or that happens in the world, whether 'good' or 'bad' (an emotionally difficult, if not impossible position to sustain, surely), or else it could mean humanity's own ability to create an earthly paradise.

That this dream has not so far materialised is not, of course, to say that it never will. But to hope that it will be realised is to part company with the Christian understanding of hope, which does not spring from confidence in the world's or humanity's own resources, but is rather rooted in a belief in the redemptive will of the benevolent, transcendent God who has called the world into existence. The world by itself, as the seventeenth-century Spanish Jesuit thinker, Baltasar Gracián, remarked and as the traditional Christian formulation *creatio ex nihilo* itself suggests, is nothing. Zero. But if taken in conjunction with God, it can amount to a great deal. This is one of the consolations of being a zero.

Is Christianity life-affirming?[3]

'What does it profit a man to gain the whole world, and lose his own soul?' Jesus asks in the gospels (Mk 8:36). 'Here we have no abiding city,' we read in the Letter to the Hebrews (Heb 13:14). 'I want no more of what men call life,' wrote Ignatius of Antioch, one of early Christianity's most reputable witnesses, literally, in his *Epistle to the Romans* (§8). The Middle Ages, for their part, are saturated with works on the theme of contempt for, or flight from, the world. Indeed the very notion of 'worldliness' is suspect in traditionally

Christian cultures. And, last but not least, the idea of renouncing worldly joys, of abandoning house and home or the possibility of founding a family of one's own 'for the sake of the kingdom of heaven' (cf. Mt 19:12, 29), has in the course of Christian history been seen as not merely compatible with, but as the most authentic expression of, Christian faith.

Faced with such a battery of evidence about the nature of Christianity, evidence that could be extended almost ad *infinitum,* those who would maintain the contrary would appear to have the burden of proof on their shoulders. Yet the contrary is now in fact being asserted, and from the highest positions in the Catholic world. Christianity, we are now assured, is life-affirming. Does this apparent volte-face on the part of church leaders represent a radically new interpretation of the Christian faith? Or does it signify that what for so long seemed to be a world-denying, resolutely ascetical faith is, when *really* understood, not world-denying at all? The answers to these questions are not immediately obvious. But what does seem to be beyond doubt is that criticisms of Christianity made since the Enlightenment – which was itself, of course, no friend of asceticism – are beginning to bear fruit.

Moved, even stung, by the critique of a world-denying, flesh-tormenting religion mounted by thinkers like Feuerbach and, especially, Nietzsche, or by men of letters such as Rilke, Christian leaders have been reassessing how they should present Christianity to an increasingly sceptical world. In this task, they undoubtedly have strong cards to play, which they don't even have to go outside the Christian tradition to seek. Rather, all that is needed to endorse the life-affirming nature of Christianity lies deeply embedded within the Christian tradition itself. First and foremost, perhaps, there is Christianity's own doctrine of creation (taken over from Judaism), which speaks of God finding his work of creation 'good,' not, as the Gnostics were to claim, a catastrophe or a 'fall'. And the sacramental, anti-iconoclastic dimension of Catholic Christianity hardly needs to be laboured. Hence the view of a Catholic sceptic, George Santayana, may be closer to the truth of Christianity than any pessimistic account of its meaning. In *Soliloquies in England and Later Soliloquies*, Santayana wrote: 'Christ loved the world, in an erotic sense in which Buddha did not love it: and the world has loved the cross as it can never love the Bo-tree.'[4] That, of course, still leaves unanswered the question of how Christianity came to be associated with a grim view of life to begin with.

This question may, in the long run, be of even more interest than the issue of how 'life-affirming' or not Christianity may actually be. For a recurrent theme of human history appears to be the way in which human beings have a knack of achieving the opposite of what they seem to have set out to achieve. Early Genesis, for instance, has God announcing that 'it is not good for man to be alone'. Hence he gave the first man, Adam, a partner, called Eve. Sexual companionship was thus conceived of as a blessing; yet human beings often manage to turn it into a curse.

To take another, and totally unrelated, example of the phenomenon mentioned: at the birth of the modern age, when belief in God was beginning to wobble, the 'Father of Modern Philosophy', René Descartes, set out to make religious belief sturdier than ever, basing his philosophy on methodical doubt. The result was a huge boost for deism and a huge blow against Christianity, which, we may charitably assume, Descartes was interested in supporting, and a not insignificant contribution to the emergence of atheism in the West, contrary entirely to Descartes' own intentions. The latest spectacular back-firing of good intentions was the emergence of communism in recent centuries, which sought paradise and discovered hell.

While it would surely be perverse to suggest that the pursuit of evil intentions might, paradoxically, be more conducive to the promotion of human happiness, the failure, or at least faltering, of good intentions should make us pause perhaps before declaring too self-confidently what exactly we think Christianity is supposed to be able to achieve.

OTHERNESS[5]

Martin Heidegger notoriously fostered the idea of truth (*aletheia*) as 'Being' revealing or 'unveiling' itself in the world of humanity. 'Meaning' or 'truth' is revealed, not reached by argument. One might call this a way of viewing truth as inherent in reality, and capable of manifesting itself in an epiphany, albeit that for Heidegger, 'it is the very fact that one is *outside* that makes possible the revelation of truth or meaning'.[6] Similarly, structuralist theory sees meaning as inherent in the different systems it observes (e.g. linguistic, social, or cultural) and as manifesting itself in the ways the various elements in such systems interrelate.

As against such theories that propose an 'internal solution' to the grand question of 'meaning', one could cite other approaches that find no such 'internal solution' to the riddle of understanding any aspect of reality. The world remains permanently opaque, permanently incomprehensible. 'Being' does not reveal itself, or articulate itself, or become itself. What instead is offered by such approaches is a belief in an 'external solution' to the incomprehensibility of the world, 'external' to the world itself, though clearly not 'external' to the divine creator.

The difference between any 'internal' and any 'external' solution to the enigma of the world lies in the belief that truth – the truth that alone is of vital interest to us – is not so much a buried treasure to be hit upon within the confines of creation or a synonym for the laws of nature, in any or all of its branches, but is rather a connection between the world of the divine and the world of the creature. In recent times, Emmanuel Lévinas ('from Being to the Other') has, in the notion of 'otherness', highlighted the alternative to a fixation on 'Being'. Not entirely surprising is his Jewish background, which he shares with many other recent figures, such as Martin Buber, who also stressed in their thinking the dialectical or 'dialogical' principle, as it is often somewhat paradoxically termed, rather than any monistic rationalism. Not entirely surprising, because for Judaism, even more (seemingly) radically than for Christianity, God is other than and cannot be confused with his creation. Which still leaves God intact, and our world intact as his creation, and the possibility of a connection between the two.

If one accepts this sense of truth, there is naturally a price to be paid, which is that one will never know fully either this world or God, either here or anywhere else. Since, however, reality transcends understanding, it is presumably unaffected by our cognitive 'gridlock', and indeed may come to be seen as growing in attractiveness for this very reason. This should not be interpreted, needless to say, as an appeal to give up on reason or to glory in confusion. It is just another sign that the innocence of truth transcends even the cunning of reason.

The Doctrine of Creation in the Theology of Karl Barth[7]

It is no secret that the star of the Swiss Protestant theologian, Karl Barth, has begun to wane in recent decades. But even currently invisible stars may, in principle, still have much light to shed on ancient, intractable problems. Science can no doubt be a useful dialogue partner for some areas of theology, but when it comes to the crunch of theodicy (or the attempt to cope with the problems caused by the existence evil for belief in the God of Christianity) Barth's intuitions about the meaning of 'creation' may perhaps still be more realistic than any amount of speculation about the 'big bang'.

Karl Barth's thought is closely associated with the complete rejection of natural theology (i.e. the attempt to bypass revelation in elaborating one's notion of God), and hence with any purely rational approach to the doctrine of creation. Rather than lamenting the shortcomings – from a Catholic point of view – of such an uncompromising approach to matters theological, it might be more helpful, initially at least, to consider Barth's positive understanding of creation. A useful summary of this can be found in chapters eight and nine of his *Dogmatics in Outline*,[8] the text of a series of lectures delivered in Bonn in the summer of 1946.

Barth rejects the idea that the doctrine of creation could be somehow easier to understand or more accessible to us than any other aspect of the creed. In his view it is false to imagine that we do not need to rely as much on revelation in dealing with creation as we do in dealing with other articles of faith. It is not, in other words, as if Christians needed revelation to discover, for example, the doctrine of the Trinity, but could work out by human reasoning alone that the world is God's creation.

> [I]t is not the existence of the world in its manifoldness, from which we are to read off the fact that God is its creator. The world with its sorrow and its happiness will always be a dark mirror to us, about which we may have optimistic or pessimistic thoughts; but it gives us no information about God as the creator. But always, when man has tried to read the truth from sun, moon and stars or from himself, the result has been an idol.[9]

For Barth the great mystery of creation lies not, as we might automatically be inclined to think, in providing a religious solution to man's search for meaning in the universe. Creation, for him, is not the church's answer to human uncertainty about the ultimate origins and destiny of the universe, i.e. the church's answer to the question, 'Is there a God who is responsible for bringing the world into existence and sustaining it?' Rather, the fundamental mystery of creation lies not in affirming that God the creator exists, but rather it lies in affirming that *we*, his creatures, exist. 'How,' Barth asks, 'can there be something alongside God, of which He has no need? This is the riddle of creation.'[10] The answer to the riddle, according to Barth, is that creation is grace.[11] God allows heaven and earth and us to exist not by necessity but by grace.

> God does not grudge the existence of the reality distinct from Himself; He does not grudge it its own reality, nature and freedom. The existence of the creature alongside God is the great puzzle and miracle, the great question to which we must and may give an answer, the

answer given us through God's Word; it is the genuine question about existence, which is essentially and fundamentally distinguished from the question which rests upon error, 'Is there a God?' That there is a world is the most unheard-of thing, the miracle of the grace of God.[12]

Barth distinguishes creation as grace from all types of gnosis, ancient and modern, which hold 'that what the Bible calls the Son is fundamentally the created world or that the world is by nature God's child'.[13] In Barth's theology, therefore, it is consistent for him to say that reason cannot bring us to the point of concluding that the world is God's creation, since creation for Barth is grace, and grace is beyond reason.

Another motive Barth has for excluding any philosophical approach to creation is that he sees creation and covenant as completely interrelated, as implying one another. Indeed, for Barth, creation takes place for the sake of the covenant. The covenant expresses the primordial truth in the God–man relationship:

[W]e would not have said the last decisive word about creation, if we did not add that the covenant between God and man is the meaning and the glory, the ground and the goal of heaven and earth and so of the whole creation … [I]t is not the case that the covenant between God and man is so to speak a second fact, something additional, but the covenant is as old as creation itself. When the existence of creation begins, God's dealing with man also begins … The covenant is not only quite as old as creation; it is older than it. Before the world was, before heaven and earth were, the resolve or decree of God exists in view of this event in which God willed to hold communion with man, as it became inconceivably true and real in Jesus Christ. And when we ask about the meaning of existence and creation, about their ground and goal, we have to think of this covenant between God and man.[14]

Barth's theological system, in particular his rejection of natural theology, is nowadays in eclipse, or at the very least one can say that it is not nearly as influential or as highly respected as it once was. His comprehensive reliance on revelation as the only true source of knowledge about God and about God's works tends now to be dismissed as an arbitrary, uncritical and thus indefensible form of biblical or ecclesiastical positivism. Because of his unwillingness to recognise any natural path leading from the world to God, he is even considered to have unwittingly helped prepare the way for the destruction of Christian faith by critical reason. However, before rejecting Barth as a fideist, it might be helpful to recall the objections to Christianity that he was trying to outflank in his own theology. It might also be apposite in this context to recall the order in which Christian truth would appear to be attained or accepted both in human experience and in the biblical witness itself.

First, what were the difficulties Barth was attempting to counter? These can be summed up under two headings: the projection theory of religion (Ludwig Feuerbach) and the problem of evil. By setting his face firmly against any attempt to extrapolate from human experience of the world to God, and by locating the mystery of creation not in God primarily but rather in the reality of the world, which exists for no reason reason can fathom, Barth aims at undercutting the whole force of Feuerbach's objection to Christianity. To this end he agrees with Feuerbach that any humanly projected God is indeed an idol, arguing that God is not the goal of man's dreams but man the result of God's grace. As for the problem of evil, this problem will always be a stumbling block on pure reason's path to God. Hence, Barth starts with faith and revelation, abandoning any pretence of being able to argue rationally from the world to the existence of God the creator. Furthermore, he links creation inextricably with the covenant (God's salvific will for humanity revealed fully in Christ). In this way, Barth is able to avoid any obviously crushing blow to his theology from the side of the problem of evil, whereas this problem would appear to be insuperable for any purely rational theodicy.

A further strength of Barth's theology of creation lies in how it dovetails with the way Christianity seems to be discerned or attained in human experience and in the record of the Bible itself. For it is a conviction or an intuition about redemption or salvation that is surely of primary importance for religious believers. From such a conviction they may, if they wish to, go on to speak about creation as implied in any belief about redemption. People, however, rarely retain or lose their faith in God, depending on the answers they may receive to abstract questions about the origins of things. Rather, they find first of all, or fail to find, life good or endurable or valuable or lovable or meaningful or worth living, and only subsequently may they come to accept that the God who has made life worthwhile must also have created it. In other words, the ultimate source of the goodness of life must also be the ultimate source of its existence.

Why, however, it might be asked, not just say that the world needs no explanation beyond itself, or that an 'internal solution' to the riddle of the world ought to be perfectly adequate? This very position has, of course, often been maintained. Thus, in Proust we read: 'It has even been said that the highest praise of God consists in the denial of him by the atheist who finds creation so perfect that he can dispense with a creator.'[15] To this exquisite paradox one can perhaps only respond somewhat helplessly by referring to the murkiness, cruelty and unfinished nature of life which seem to preclude any straightforward acceptance of its intrinsic wholeness or self-sufficiency, now or at any other point along the path of history. For even a possibly glowing future for humanity and the world could never of itself be reason enough to justify or redeem the horrors of the past. It must be conceded, however, that the permanent human refusal to justify such horrors is an expression of faith; it is not based on any appeal to a self-evident situation of fact or to a self-grounding set of 'values'. And as such, it springs – as, presumably, all faith ultimately must – from hope in the transcendent goodness of God who cannot condone evil and who, Christianity teaches, will be vindicated as the Redeemer at the end of time.

Thus it would seem, for instance, to be the case that the Israelites experienced the shortcomings and painfulness of existence, and in consequence perceived God first and foremost as a redeemer and only subsequently as a creator, and not vice versa. The Book of Job is a powerful, if still ambiguous, example of this process. And in the New Testament, Jesus is seen primarily as the redeemer or saviour and only secondarily as the mediator of creation. It is interesting to find the same priority given to existential as opposed to factual – or, one might even say, scientific – questions by Theodor Adorno, when he writes on the question of the value of philosophical knowledge:

> The only form of philosophy which could be justified in the face of despair, is the attempt to see everything in the perspective of redemption. Knowledge has no light other than that which shines from redemption onto the world. Everything else is empty and imitative, sheer technical effects.[16]

In short, knowledge – whether knowledge of creation or of anything else – is only of use, to put it in religious terms, in so far as it is salvific or redemptive for human existence. When knowledge of the world has no reference beyond itself, it can seem pointless. For its part, theology, as a discipline, is of course no better placed in this respect than any other intellectual activity. If theology has no reference beyond itself, if it becomes an end in itself, it inevitably becomes sterile. It only begins to live when or if it seems to be assisting people to cope with the human predicament, even if – indeed, perhaps, only if – this is not its self-conscious or deliberate primary aim. Its first aim can only ever be to seek and speak the truth.

Whether or not we find Barth convincing on creation – and on the role reason can or cannot play in convincing us of the truth of the doctrine of creation – is a question we should probably not wish to answer too hastily. It would certainly be foolish to dust down as sly a thinker as Barth, and then dismiss him for being – in any crude sense – irrational or uncritical.

Is Christianity Unnatural?[17]

It is, I think, interesting to note that the season of Lent gets its *name* at least not from any specifically Christian or even religious notion, but from an Old English word for spring. It's a word that's thought to be connected with the idea of length, hence with the time when the days begin to lengthen, as happens in the spring. Now usually we tend to imagine Lent as a serious, solemn, even joyless, and penitential time of year, in theory at any rate, a time when we're urged to take on various kinds of penance, and try to deny ourselves some of the physical pleasures of life in order to improve the state of our spiritual life. Exercises of self-denial – or, as it used to be called, mortification of the body and its appetites and passions – were supposed to help tame the selfish appetites of the flesh and make the life of the soul thereby healthier. But the season of spring seems far removed from any notion of self-denial or mortification. It conjures up almost exactly the opposite kind of reality. Spring is the season when nature comes back to life again after appearing to have been almost dead all through the winter. It's a season, therefore, that would seem to be more in tune with ideas of self-development, self-realisation, self-fulfilment even, rather than with potentially gloomy thoughts about self-denial or self-sacrifice.

So why, in what should be a joyful, even exhilarating period of the year's natural cycle, does the church see fit to locate the season of Lent? What message is being conveyed by this choice, by this juxtaposition or coincidence of nature's rebirth with the church's most urgent invitation to us in the year to practise at least for the forty days of Lent some kind of self-renunciation or self-denial? Does this not just go to show yet again how unnatural, how even inherently inhuman Christianity fundamentally is? That certainly has been an accusation frequently levelled at the Christian church, and not just in modern times. And when one considers some of the more extreme penances Christians have been tempted to inflict on themselves over the centuries, there is perhaps a grain of truth in such accusations.

But the grain of truth may also point in a more promising direction. For while there may be some truth in the suspicion that Christianity is unnatural, it's equally important, indeed maybe it's even more important, to see that being 'unnatural' is not such a bad thing. At least not for humanity. Human beings are not locked into nature in the way other species are. In that sense we are not just part of nature, we aren't purely 'natural'. Animals can't deliberately change their way of behaving or alter the way they react to their environment; human beings can. We can change our minds; we can have second thoughts about things (which presumably is what 'metanoia' means); we can be changed by the grace of God.

So perhaps the wisdom of the church's choice of spring as the Lenten season lies in the need to remind us, lest we forget – as we are inevitably prone to do in this busy, demanding and distracting world – that there is a discrepancy between our rhythms and the rhythms of nature. Spring ushers in year by year the rebirth or reawakening of nature, but the rebirth we need isn't so predictable or so accessible. Indeed, the very coming of spring can even cruelly underline for many people the difference between the burgeoning, blossoming state of nature all around them and the desolation of their own mind and heart. 'When will my spring come?' is the last line of an ancient Latin poem, written by someone who was clearly acutely aware of the divergence between nature's newly found life and his own inner barrenness. In that sense, in diverting our attention away from nature and towards another reality in the season of Lent, the church, far from being condemned or chided for being unnatural and inhuman, should perhaps be seen rather as supremely human and supremely compassionate and supremely realistic. For Christianity, despite all it knows about the human condition, still does hold out belief in the possibility of rebirth and new life for humanity, but it's a rebirth and a new life that doesn't come from nature. It builds on nature, certainly, but it doesn't come from nature. It comes from God.

This, I think, is the real message of the transfiguration and the reason why the church has the account of the transfiguration read in the season of Lent, and in fact on the same Sunday, the second Sunday of Lent, in all three liturgical years. Yet transfiguration is not straightforward. The bad news is that a transfiguration of the world cannot last within the confines of history, desperately though we may wish for this, as Peter, John and James seem to have done in this morning's gospel. We, as human beings, don't seem to have the capacity to endure the reality of transfiguration for too long on this earth, as Jesus' brief transfiguration suggests, and certainly we don't seem either to have the ability to transfigure the world ourselves. Indeed, one of the most poignant and terrible ironies of recent history is that a kind of diabolical transfiguration of reality was effected by human beings on the actual date of the feast of the transfiguration, on 6 August 1945, when the first atomic bomb, with all its dazzling and devastating power, was dropped on a civilian population, on Hiroshima, transfiguring it and the people within it in a way that will never be forgotten as long as history lasts.

If the bad news is that we can't transfigure ourselves, the good news is that we still can be transfigured or changed by the grace of God. But, as the second reading today reminds us, that transfiguration will only be complete in our homeland in heaven where we hope that Christ 'will transfigure these wretched bodies of ours into copies of his glorious body'. In renouncing any definitive fulfilment in this life – which is the hard road Lent encourages us to take – we still leave open the possibility of finding 'God in the wilderness of life'[18] and the hope of being led by the Spirit of God to the fullness of divine glory in heaven.

DOES LOVING GOD MEAN HATING THE WORLD?[19]

The word 'life' or 'world' occurs in today's gospel reading, but it seems to have two different meanings. Jesus speaks about people either loving or hating their life in this world, and he also speaks about 'the eternal life'. And if we ask what is the connection or the relation between life in this world and the eternal life, the answer seems to be contained in Jesus' saying that 'anyone who hates his life in this world will keep it for the eternal world'.

But when we think about this, it must strike us as a bit odd. The God who was in Jesus is the God, we believe, who also created this world and ourselves. And if God created this world, why should we hate it? Surely we should love it and be grateful for it? Similarly, when parents bring children into the world, they surely don't do so for their children to hate this world. That would amount to hating their parents as well. So, when Jesus talks about hating the world, he can't mean this to be taken literally. What, then, does he mean?

The answer would appear to lie in something else Jesus says in another part of today's gospel. 'Unless a wheat grain falls on the ground and dies, it remains only a single grain, but if it dies, it yields a rich harvest.' This line seems to give us the clue we need to understand what Jesus really means when he talks about hating this world. He means that this life is a gift from God, but that it can only really blossom and become something even greater if we accept it as a gift with open hands and share it with others, rather than trying to close our hands on it and grasp it and keep it for ourselves. In other words, if we love the world, in the sense of wanting to possess it only for ourselves, we will be unable to use it for the good of others, and will even ruin it in the end for ourselves as well. We all know the dangers of being a miser. A miser, by keeping everything to himself, enriches no one, and as the word suggests becomes miserable himself, finding no happiness in the life he wishes to keep only for himself.

When our hands are closed possessively on life, when our fists are clenched, we can't give anything, but neither can we receive or accept anything; we can't help anyone, nor can we embrace or caress anything or anyone. At most, clenched fists can be used to hit people and hurt them, and so add to the sum of the world's suffering.

And yet, Jesus isn't just giving us a moral message about how we should live in this world, important though that undoubtedly is. But beyond that, he is telling us something even more significant. He is saying that God is capable not just of giving us life, as we know from our presence here on this earth, but he is also assuring us that if we can cooperate generously and open-handedly with God in this world, or in his own words, if we can hate this world in the sense of hating any grasping possessiveness with regard to life in this world, then God can turn our lives, even despite death, into a reflection of his very own divine, eternal life, here already in this world to some extent, and in fullness in the world to come, where we can enjoy life with God for ever.

CREATION AND ITS DISCONTENTS[20]

On the occasion of the World Day of the Sick, it might be appropriate to think for a few moments about why the church has always seen fit to highlight the importance of the sick, even to the extent of seeing them as the privileged recipients of one of the seven sacraments, the Anointing of the Sick, which the healthy, of course, are not eligible to receive.

But in asking why Christianity considers the sick to have a special place in the world, we are treading on delicate terrain. Even to pose the question may be the wrong thing to do, because it sets up a potentially dubious or at least tasteless and even condescending dichotomy between the healthy and the sick. The presumption is that the healthy can examine the sick, and in a certain sense sit in judgement on them, as though the sick were in some sense inferior to the healthy.

On the other hand, there is no point either, I think, in glamorising or glorifying or sentimentalising sickness and suffering, or saying smugly, for example, that the sick and the suffering are closer to God than the healthy. Because I suspect that the sick don't want to hear this; they want, rather, to be healthy again. And even though Christianity has often been accused of it, I don't think that true Christianity relishes the prospect of seeing as much sickness and suffering in the world as possible, as if sickness and suffering were somehow welcome forces that make people easier or softer targets for evangelisation. It's surely distasteful to try to get at people when they're down. And indeed, if we look at the picture of Jesus that emerges from the gospels, we'll see that he was concerned to heal illness and alleviate suffering, not exploit it in order to frighten or otherwise force people into taking a keener interest in God. There is no evidence, as far as I know, that Jesus ever interpreted serious illness or other disasters that befall human beings as, say, divine punishment for sin, or as useful educational tricks God kept up his sleeve to use on certain people in order to keep them on the 'straight and narrow'.

And yet, the traditional accusations against Christianity in relation to illness and suffering are maybe not entirely without foundation. Or at least it's fairly easy to see why Christianity has been accused or can be accused of exalting sickness and suffering over health, or even death over life, because, considered superficially, Christianity seems in the course of its history to have spent quite a considerable amount of energy reminding people about the certainty of death for everyone and of its ever-present threat, whereas it seems to have spoken less confidently and less forthrightly about, say, the beauty of the world, or the 'pride of life' (1 Jn 2:16), or the pleasures life has to offer. According to as representative a figure as Pascal, 'sickness is the natural state of a Christian'.[21] So it's perhaps not surprising if Christianity has sometimes been charged with seeing the whole world as a 'vale of tears' (as the Hail Holy Queen has it), or as a kind of vast hospital where we, the patients, wait until our own turn comes to face our final illness. This lugubrious view of human existence that Christianity is supposed to have espoused, a view that tends to portray life itself as a kind of disease or disaster, is, of course, something of a caricature, but a caricature only exaggerates for effect something that is fundamentally characteristic of a person or, in this case, a religion.

And it is indeed true that Christianity has constantly reminded us that our lives here on this earth are always encompassed by the threat of suffering and the certainty of death, but it has also taught that both life and death are encompassed by God, who is master of both. So, the sometimes glibly made remark that God is especially close to the sick is true to the extent that in sickness and particularly in the face of death people may gain a more acute awareness of the limited, finite and transitory nature of their lives, and so of all human life. But by the same token they may also gain a keener insight into the incomparable value and beauty of existence. These two things aren't contradictory. On the contrary. It's maybe only because life is finite, only because we know we have to leave it, that it can be experienced as so uniquely desirable. Even heaven, according to Christian faith, won't have the disturbing but yet invigorating uncertainties that give life on earth its special savour. The fact, however, that we have to depart this life means that we don't own it, and so its attractiveness and its beauty can't belong to us, or can't come from within us; they must have another source, a source that is beyond us, and this source we call God.

The paradox is, then, that what we don't own or possess, namely life itself, is infinitely more valuable than any particular thing at all that we can own or that we can do within this life. And similarly, none of the evils or the suffering of life that we may experience or even be responsible for ourselves is necessarily capable, our faith tells us, of undermining or rendering null and void the fundamental value and goodness of God's creation. Life, in short, is always redeemable, and by God's grace, we believe, can always be redeemed.

It's important, though, to see that the value of life, for Christianity, doesn't come from us or from anything else in the world: there is too much sadness and pain in the world and too much potential for evil within ourselves for us to simply decree life as infinitely valuable. Life, Christianity believes, is only valuable if taken in conjunction with God, somewhat in the way a word can have meaning only within, or in conjunction with, a language. In short, it is only because life, as Christianity teaches, is created and redeemed (or endorsed) by the living God that it is eternally valuable. By being our creator and identifying himself, in Christ, with the world of human pain, God guarantees the everlasting value of this life and even of human suffering. Thus even suffering, in God's dispensation, is finally not only not allowed to undermine the reality of our salvation, but, in some incomprehensible way, is even compelled by God to contribute to that salvation.

ORIGINAL SIN AND THE ENLIGHTENMENT

It is often argued that the Enlightenment was an all-out attack on Christianity. To the extent that Christianity can be identified exclusively with the church, there is some truth to this contention. Voltaire's repeated adage of *Écrasez l'infâme*[22] would certainly appear to support it. Yet many Enlightenment thinkers, including Voltaire himself, were in no sense atheists. What the Enlightenment most objected to in Christianity was not at all its belief in God, or even its singling out of the significance of Jesus (provided, of course, this was restricted to seeing Jesus as a moral teacher and exemplar of the lived moral life). What the Enlightenment most repudiated in Christianity was, in fact, its doctrine of original sin, and hence its view of redemption.

Indeed the Enlightenment's attitude towards the doctrine of original sin was pivotal to the overall thrust and intention of that whole complex movement. As John McManners has written: 'The essential, unifying conviction of the Enlightenment, Cassirer has emphasised, was the rejection of the idea of original sin.'[23] In a later, more general survey of the impact of the Enlightenment on European culture, McManners notes:

> The writers of the Enlightenment were sapping the weakest buttress of Christian doctrine when they attacked the concept of original sin. The arguments for its transmission were improbable or dubiously ethical, and for its imputation, unethical altogether. As Voltaire pointed out, cab horses are whipped, but it is not rational or moral to suppose that this is because one of them had once eaten forbidden oats.[24]

The Catholic church, needless to say, in its official teaching capacity rejected the Enlightenment's attitude to original sin, and was in turn dismissed by the Enlightenment as hopelessly out of tune with reality, and even anti-human.[25] For the Enlightenment did not wish to accept the idea of a humanly irremovable imperfectibility in life. Leszek Kolakowski has summarised lucidly what was at stake in this clash, and why the Enlightenment made the choice it did, against the Christian church:

> By making people acutely aware of their contingency and the finitude of life, of the corruptibility of the body, of the limitations of reason and language, of the power of evil in us, and by concentrating this awareness in the doctrine of original sin, Christianity clearly defied the Promethean side of the Enlightenment and was to be inevitably castigated for its 'anti-humanist' bias.[26]

In the short run, Christianity, with its continued championing of original sin, was left defending what, in the heyday of the

Enlightenment, was culturally a fairly hopeless cause. And it seems beyond dispute that belief in the doctrine of original sin did in fact decline dramatically in the post-Enlightenment world. The Enlightenment's critique of the doctrine of original sin is, furthermore, perhaps ultimately more significant in trying to explain the decline in belief in the doctrine in recent centuries, than the problems raised for the teaching by modern evolutionary theory, or the rise of historical consciousness, or even the development of modern biblical criticism. At bottom, the conflict between traditional Christianity and the Enlightenment, which was at its most acute in the opposed views they held on the question of 'original sin', is a recrudescence of the far older conflict between grace and free will (or 'works') that marked, say, the dispute between St Augustine and Pelagius in a much earlier period of church history. And one might also argue that the modern dispute was to a significant degree inevitable, or at the very least not unexpected, as an understandable reaction against the intense pessimism about human existence that characterised many of the Reformers in the age that preceded the Enlightenment.

Seen in the longer perspective of history, the modern difficulties encountered by the Christian doctrine of original sin cannot, in my view, be credibly tackled by exclusive appeals to modern biblical criticism, for all that the latter may be able to cast new light on, for instance, the real meaning of St Paul's often misunderstood parallel between Adam and Christ in Romans 5. Even more sophisticated readings of the opening chapters of the Bible, with their narratives of creation and the origin of sin in human history, will most likely not, of themselves, shed too much light on the question of the meaning of 'original sin' for Christianity, if such readings focus only or mainly on the question of the 'historicity' of the 'Adam and Eve' story.

Nor is much help with the sense of the early texts of Genesis to be expected, I would guess, from 'dialogue', as it is sometimes termed, with the natural sciences. This is not in any sense to disparage the latter, which theology has clearly no right or competence to do. It is simply to suggest that early Genesis is not in fact an attempt to describe convincingly how the world emerged and developed. Rather, it seems to be a poetic creation aimed at placing the ambiguities and inadequacies of human experience in relation to faith in God. It is, in other words, about delineating, or striving to delineate, the 'uncontrollable mystery' of human freedom and hope, while at the same time respecting the inscrutable mystery of God, and indeed seeing the former as uniquely related to the latter.

What the story of 'Adam and Eve' is trying to convey – mainly by way of the narrative of the 'Fall' (a term not actually used in the biblical text),[27] since no purely rational explanation of the issues involved is adequate or, by implication, possible – is that human history (and to this extent, the traditional insistence on the 'historicity' of Adam and Eve does have an important point to make) is not lived out in paradise, but neither is it pointless or aimless. It still does, despite the (inevitable?) presence of evil, have a goal, or, in perhaps more theological language, it still does have a wider or deeper redemptive context, assured by the creator. Whatever about the problems caused for Adam and Eve by the 'tree of the knowledge of good and evil', the other tree (the 'tree of life') is still intact and thus can still possibly be reached. How, we are not quite sure, as the Book of Genesis doesn't tell us.

For Christianity, the human race is caught between the impossibility of reaching happiness unaided, and the equally real impossibility of giving up on the quest for happiness definitively. Original sin, which frustrates the achievement of human happiness in any deliberately planned, self-made, Pelagian way, and the indeterminate nature of man ('made in the image of God'), which leaves open the possibility of endless human striving for happiness, these twin constants of existence together account for the eternal recurrence of tragedy in human history: '*Es irrt der Mensch, so lang er strebt*', as Goethe's well-known line has it.[28]

Just as important, however, as seeing original sin in the light of redemption, perhaps even more so is to see original sin in the light of the doctrine of creation. For, to see original sin in the context of creation is to give it its true significance, which is to point to man's inextricable link with God, no matter what happens in history. For those who have eyes to see, that link – since we believe God is good –

will be experienced, more often than not, as a 'falling short' of the glory of God. *That* is the Fall, and not some pre-cosmic or pre-historical catastrophe, which we were helpless to prevent and for which we must forever be punished.

But to 'fall short' is still to be dimly aware of the goodness not just that lies ahead, but that underlies and surrounds everything. That this goodness is obviously not our possession, even when we sense it, is why it has usually in Christian tradition been referred to as grace. And that grace doesn't cease to be, simply because we don't possess it, is the 'reason' why it is reasonable to hope in redemption. The relief of knowing that there is something to fall short of is perhaps the meaning of religious peace. The suspicion that the 'falling short' will be eternal, that we are doomed to share the fate of Tantalus, may cloud that peace, but cannot destroy it. Sufficient unto the universe is the clarity thereof, even if it is a 'cloud of unknowing'.

This universe in which our lives unfold reveals its value, not its worthlessness, in the light of original sin. The sadness of human history would make no sense if human life were of no significance. For, life's significance is – paradoxically – underlined, not undermined, by the potential for suffering our decisions can unleash. This awesome discovery – narrated paradigmatically by the author of Genesis – is re-enacted by the great masters of Tragedy, but it clearly goes beyond the scope of mere discursive prose to explain. For Christian faith, the beauty of original sin lies in its being an oblique demonstration of the indestructible value of that creation in which we 'live and move and have our being', and also in its being the key which opens the gate out of Paradise and sets humanity on the hard road to Heaven.[29]

THE DOCTRINE OF GOD

How Grim is God?[1]

It would be difficult, I think, to have any doubts at all about the deep religious faith of John the Baptist, who figures prominently in today's gospel reading, or any doubts about the sincerity and energy he showed in living out that faith. He seems to have been a person with a very black and white picture of reality, which included having a rather low opinion of the moral standards and political conditions of his country, an unwillingness to be a part of normal society any longer, and an unshakeable conviction that God wasn't going to let this state of affairs continue much longer without making his disapproval felt in some final cataclysmic act of judgement on the world. That's why we find John the Baptist in this morning's reading out in the wilderness, somewhat eccentrically clad, following a very frugal diet, and calling on people to repent while there was still time.

John was certainly a strong personality, but also rather gloomy and harsh, someone who may even have relished the task of delivering his dire warnings. He's not the sort of person you could imagine at a party or a whist drive, say. He comes across as a very forbidding figure and prompts the question: if repentance means becoming as gloomy and as grim as John the Baptist, is it not nearly better to remain a sinner? Or to put it another way: since repentance is a good idea, does it necessarily have to lead to grimness and severity? The New Testament suggests, I think, not. The New Testament never for a moment *denies* the greatness of John, who lived out his own vocation to the point of martyrdom. Indeed some of his followers even considered him to be the Messiah. Yet the gospels identify Jesus, not John, as the Messiah. We should ask: why? Or to put the same question slightly differently: why was Jesus the Messiah not like John, or at least not more like John? What was it about Jesus that placed him above John? What was the Holy Spirit that John mentions in today's gospel, but that only Jesus and not John was able to give, a Spirit that evidently drew people to Jesus more emphatically than to John? Now, it's all very well to say that Jesus was divine, and John for all his religious greatness wasn't. But how does divinity manifest itself over and above the religious teaching and example of John the Baptist?

Part of the answer seems to lie in the fact that Jesus didn't see the world in such black and white terms as John. Jesus too preached repentance, but gave more of a breathing space to sinners to repent than John and even suggested that while God didn't actually approve of wrong-doing, he for some mysterious reason treated the just and unjust equally, letting the rain fall and the sun shine on all, without distinction. A more radical interpretation of this attitude is to see it as somewhat ironical, since as St Paul put it, 'all fall short of the glory of God', hence *all* really are sinners and merit destruction, but God holds back. Why does he hold back, why did he not bring the world to an end as John the Baptist anticipated, as even the early Christians expected? The answer must include the truth that God is different from our views of him or our expectations of him. He's not predictable and doesn't always do what is expected or secretly desired of him. Hence he's not boring and is perhaps partly for that reason worth having hope in.

Yet hope, real hope, is impossible without the possibility of failure and despair, just as victory in anything is worthless without the possibility of defeat. You can't enjoy swimming without taking the risk of drowning. Life is unfortunately real,[2] and the risks involved in living are real too. Hope, it has been said, is a great falsifier of truth. But that's only the case if hope is equated with optimism and allowed to blind us to the great and banal truths about our limitations and our inevitable mortality, that is to say: to original sin.

Traditional Christian hope has never been of the thoughtless, superficial variety. Rather it has been clear-sighted, even ruthlessly frank at times, about what human beings can expect from themselves or from each other on this earth. But it has always pointed beyond all this to the unknown side of God and encouraged the faithful to keep faith with their unpredictable God.

A great poet of the Middle Ages, Dante Alighieri, was able to conceive of the whole human venture, of all human life, as a divine comedy. You may not think at the moment that there's very much in the world to laugh about, but the point of a divine comedy is that there's a happy end to look forward to. It's the conviction that God will ultimately turn up trumps, even if he continues to keep most of his cards close to his chest throughout our history – it's this conviction that has sustained people down through the ages. It's this conviction that in turn allows us once again this Advent to raise our eyes anticipating the return of Christmas when the hope of the world was born.

WHY WAIT FOR GOD?[3]

Advent, as we know, is a time of expectation; it's a season whose keynote is one of waiting, waiting for the arrival of God. What we might not stress so clearly in Advent is that if we *are* genuinely waiting for something, if we *are* really looking forward to something, then that can only be because what we are at present, and who we are at present are matters that have not yet been finally settled.

The readings today reflect this contrast between what is and what could or should or might still be. The first reading from the Book of Baruch compares the 'sorrow and distress' of Jerusalem with 'the light of [God's] glory' that will one day guide Israel. The second reading from the Letter of St Paul to the Philippians contrasts the good work God has begun in the Philippians with its completion, which still lies in the future. And finally, then, in the gospel, John the Baptist, by proclaiming a baptism of repentance for the forgiveness of sins and promising that 'all mankind shall see the salvation of God', clearly realises that the world he is involved in does not represent the final state of things as God would like them to be.

Now, we might meditate on these three readings and only reach the conclusion that what they all tell us is what our common sense and even a superficial acquaintance with the history of the world would tell us anyway, namely that there always is and always has been a gulf in human existence between the way things are and the way we are, and the way we would ideally like the world and ourselves to be. This contrast between reality and desire seems to be an unchanging feature of the human scene.

The question, then, we have to ask ourselves is: 'What else, what more does Christianity, and what more, specifically, do the readings today give us or tell us that our ordinary insight into the ways of the world cannot give us?' For, if Christianity can just tell us what normal experience alone tells us anyway, then it couldn't be seriously described as 'news' at all, let alone as 'the good news', which is what the gospel claims to be. What Christianity gives us is, however, something more. What it gives us is the belief that our will to change, our wish for the world to be different from what it is, to be more just, more humane, less terrifying – that all that is not an end in itself, however desirable it may actually appear to us to be. The gospel tells us that even more is at stake in our lives than changing ourselves and changing the world – good and worthy though all that undoubtedly is. The gospel tells us is that the point of wanting to do all this is so that God may be able to find a way to us, that God may be able to reach us. What we should be waiting for in the wilderness of existence is, therefore, not only the creation of a better world, but God, who is the only one who can bring our life and ourselves to perfection and whose will it is to bring us to perfection.

Now, when we hear the expression 'the will of God', we may often, I suspect, hear it more as a threat, or an imposition, or a huge constraining force on us, keeping us down and even keeping us frightened. But for Christianity, 'the will of God' is the will that created this world and the will that was incarnate in Jesus Christ. For Christianity, God's will existed before we were created, and existed indeed before anything or anyone was created. When we realise this, we can, then, perhaps begin to understand that we are sustained and guided by a creative will that is greater than ours, a will that can bring life out of apparently dead matter – as we are told happened with our own planet – and that can be trusted to complete in all of humanity the good work begun in our creation.

Caught up, as most people are a lot of the time, in the business of surviving in the world, it is of course difficult to stand aside from the serious business of living, in order to try to see things from God's point of view. What extraordinary figures like John the Baptist claim to be doing is precisely that: they claim to be giving us a description of God's point of view. But to do that, we notice, John the Baptist had to give up everything else and head for the wilderness. Clearly not everyone can be a prophet. Happily, however, John the Baptist's message *is* for everyone, and that message is ultimately one of great consolation, because it tells us that when everything else may have been lost, when we find ourselves in whatever wilderness life may have driven us into, that even then the greatest gift of all is still available to us: God himself.

PASCAL'S GOD[4]

Modern Christian apologetics can be traced back to Pascal. Like Descartes, from whom he is otherwise so different, Pascal took seriously the new world view opened up by navigators like Columbus, astronomers like Copernicus, and the incomparable underminer of old certainties, Montaigne. For his part, Pascal sought to reinvent not philosophy, like Descartes, but rather Christianity itself, by scrutinizing the human condition candidly and showing it to be most persuasively accounted for by Christian revelation.

Does he succeed? Or does he demonstrate rather that in his beginning is his end? Are his arguments for God convincing, or does he simply glamorise human anguish? Does he make the reality of God a palpable experience, or is his defence of Christianity finally, though unforgettably, 'only' a moving evocation of humanity's invincible solitude and transience?

One writer who appears to favour the latter evaluation is Jorge Luis Borges. In an essay on Pascal he argues:

Pascal, they tell us, found God, but the way he expressed that blissful reality is less eloquent than the way he expressed the experience of solitude. In this he was incomparable ...

... Pascal affirms that nature (space) is 'an infinite sphere whose centre is everywhere and whose circumference is nowhere'... The metaphor Pascal uses to define space is employed by his predecessors[5] to define the deity. Pascal is moved not by the greatness of the Creator, but by the greatness of Creation.

... What matters to him is not so much God as the refutation of those who deny him.[6]

In a further short essay, entitled 'Pascal's Sphere', we read:

In that dispirited century, the absolute space which inspired the hexameters of Lucretius, the absolute space which had been a liberation for Bruno, was for Pascal a labyrinth and an abyss. Pascal loathed the universe and would have liked to adore God, but God, for him, was less real than the universe he loathed.[7]

Pascal's application to the universe of a metaphor reserved traditionally for God might entitle him to be regarded as an early, albeit involuntary, seculariser of Christianity, while his anguished, even despairing, vision of the universe may be an unexpected echo of the ancient Gnostic myth of the evil demiurge who created this world: two reasons why it is risky to have Pascal as a theological ally. Borges' assumption, on the other hand, that to find God is bliss places him, curiously enough, on the side of the angels.

GOD'S JUDGEMENT ON THE WORLD[8]

In today's gospel reading Jesus has some very sharp things to say to his listeners about their itch to correct and judge other people. He denounces such behaviour as hypocrisy. Jesus reminds us that to presume to judge others, you'd really have to be without spot or blemish yourself, you'd have to be pure and good, without as much as a tiny splinter of imperfection in your own life, whereas most of us have whole planks of imperfection to contend with. This boils down to the fact that only God has the right to judge, because only God is purely and completely good and just. We aren't.

Now, to speak of God as a judge conjures up the image of life itself as a sort of legal process or trial, and many people nowadays are uneasy with that sort of language. They find it unattractive and uncongenial as a way of thinking about human life. Most people nowadays, I suspect, would prefer to see life as a kind of journey or pilgrimage, but not as a legal trial. To put it in extreme terms, most of us, surely, would rather go on holiday than go to court.

But if we do turn our backs on the traditional Christian language of trial and judgement, and embrace the seemingly more reassuring notion of life as a journey, we might just be setting out on a wild-goose chase and missing out on something of great, indeed of ultimate importance that the older symbols attempt to convey.

For, traditional Christianity didn't originally speak about God as a judge, and human life here on earth as a trial, in order to frighten people about God and about their lives. The original message of Christianity is that before we set out on the trial of life, we have, at the very start, already been cleared by God of any charges against us, or – to put it in slightly different terms – the original message of Christianity is that we have passed our examination before we even set out on our course of study. It was the relief and joy of accepting this message from Jesus Christ that set people in the early church free from anxiety about God, and free from fear and foreboding about their future, and set them free then to face the inevitable burdens and sufferings of life with confidence and hope. That is why St Paul could say to the Christians of Corinth – as we heard in today's second reading – that they had no reason ever to give in or to admit defeat, because no earthly power or problem could ever undo, or take away, or undermine, or render null and void the victory won for the human race in Jesus Christ.

That victory is the judgement on the world that the Christian faith believes in. It's not a judgement to be frightened about, but on the contrary it's a judgement to celebrate, because it represents God's assessment of, or verdict on, humanity. And that verdict is that humanity is so precious in God's eyes that he sent his only Son into the world of flesh and suffering in order to unite the human race to himself. The substance of this divine verdict on human life lies in the triumph of God's power and goodness over the forces of evil in the death and resurrection of Jesus Christ. And it is this triumph that we celebrate in every mass, as we look forward in the midst of the trials of this life to the Last Judgement when the full glory of what God has done and won for us in Jesus Christ will be revealed.

THE BACK OF GOD[9]

The eighteenth-century German thinker Lichtenberg once said that the fact that sermons are preached in churches makes the presence of lightning conductors on such buildings not altogether redundant. This is a salutary warning to anyone who dares to take on the awesome task of interpreting the reality of God in the words of mere mortals. For how are we to recognise and speak about the living God in and for our own time and place? How are we to avoid misinterpreting the signs of his presence?

Today's three readings mention most of the great realities of our religion, and indeed of human existence. I'll mention just some of them, more or less as they occur: priesthood, laity, infidelity, worship, prophecy, ridicule, contempt, warfare, destruction, exile, desolation, hope, love, sin, Christ Jesus, grace, faith, eternal life, condemnation, light, darkness, evil, truth, and finally – as the last word in the readings, occurring for the twelfth time today I make it – God.

We could, I think, make some fist at understanding much of what the readings are talking about today, like war and destruction and exile and hope, which are the stuff of world news reported day in and day out in our lives. But when we move out of the sphere of those activities or passions that we might have more familiarity with than others, and try to approach realities referred to by words like grace, salvation, damnation, eternal life and, above all, God himself, we are in much less familiar territory.

And yet, if we could only understand God, all the rest would be clear. But as we know, in life we can see almost everything else, but maddeningly and frustratingly, we can't see God. There is nothing new about that of course. An ancient Christian commentator on the passage in the Bible that tells of the attempt Moses made to see God notes that Moses was only permitted to look on the back of God, and – the commentator adds – the back of God is the world. All we ever see of God or can see of God is the world itself. But faith tells us that this world is God's creation. We would need God's eyes, however, to be able actually to *see* that. Yet it is surely enough for us to *believe* that what God sees in the world is what we, because of our various types of blindness, only rarely see, namely that as the world is eminently lovable, human beings are so too.

'God loved us with so much love that he was generous with his mercy,' we hear in the letter to the Ephesians. 'Yes, God loved the world so much that he gave his only Son, so that everyone who believes in him may not be lost but may have eternal life,' says St John in his gospel. ———

God's ways are not ours, and God's eyes are certainly not ours. When we hear in the letter to the Ephesians, 'We are God's work of art,' and try to apply that statement honestly to ourselves or – dare I say it? – to our neighbours, we might be inclined to mutter: 'Some work of art ...', and think such language is just too good to be true. At such moments of grave temptation, an idea of Wittgenstein's might be worth remembering. He wrote once: 'We tend to take the speech of a Chinese for inarticulate gurgling. Someone who understands Chinese will recognise language in what he hears. Similarly I often cannot discern the humanity in a man.'[10] If we cannot discern the humanity in ourselves or in another human being, we have at least the consolation of knowing that God who made us does discern and understand and love the humanity in us, and wishes to transform and preserve it as his work of art. That is

44

the good news of the Christian faith that can always be relied on to outshine 'the perennial bad news of the human condition'.[11]

Christianity's survival over 2,000 years allows us to hope that the last word on our condition will not be left to the dark forces of human history – hinted at in today's gospel reading – that put Jesus to death, but belongs to the living God who created us and is now calling us to share in divine Glory.

We live by faith, not by knowledge. As St John expressed it in his first letter: 'We are God's children now; it does not yet appear what we shall be, but we know that when he appears we shall be like him, for we shall see him as he is.' (1 Jn 3:2)

Those words are strange and incomprehensible, but they are also consoling because they hold out to us a promise and a hope of better days, of brighter days. As the poet Louis MacNeice put it:

> ... there will be sunlight later
> And the equation will come out at last.[12]

THE 'WILL OF GOD' AND THE JUDGEMENT OF MAN[13]

In today's second reading, from the Letter to the Hebrews, we are given a piece of advice that many people might find a bit hard to swallow. We are first told that God disciplines those he loves, and then we are urged to endure our trials as 'discipline'. Now, if we are suffering in some way, or weighed down with some difficulty or problem in our lives, then we know that it can sound very glib when someone presumes to tell us at that moment: 'Oh, such things are sent to try us. We should accept them as God's will.' Quite apart from the fact that Christianity isn't about accepting things fatalistically – didn't Jesus himself try to relieve suffering where he found it, and in that way gave us encouragement also to try to ease human suffering when and where we can? – there is something in all of us, I think, that bristles at being told complacently by others, who frequently aren't suffering themselves, that we should endure whatever we have to suffer as the 'will of God'.

And the reason we bristle and take offence at this and resent it is probably very healthy: it is most likely because we instinctively realise that only God can speak about the 'will of God', not our fellow human beings, no matter how eminent they are, or how learned or how influential or how important. And interestingly enough, in the gospels Jesus, the Son of God, typically doesn't tell people to endure their sufferings as the will of God, but he reveals himself as the Lamb of God who takes the sins and sufferings of the world upon himself, for our redemption.

Now, while all that is fundamental to our Christian faith, it would still, I think, be a pity if we were to go to the opposite extreme of what I mentioned earlier and throw out entirely the idea of enduring our trials. The fact that a religious idea may have been interpreted glibly or self-interestedly or even aggressively against people, to put or keep them down or even to make them feel unnecessarily guilty, for example – that of *itself* doesn't mean to say that the idea in question is thereby completely discredited or disqualified. In other words, an idea that is falsely interpreted doesn't have to be itself necessarily false. *'Abusus non tollit usum'*,[14] to quote an ancient legal maxim.

The idea of enduring 'trials' does in fact have, I think, a profound and legitimate religious meaning, which we might more easily grasp if we were to think of a 'trial' as an 'experience'. Experience, in fact, originally meant a 'trial'; and part of that meaning is retained, indeed, in the notion of an 'experiment', which is also a kind of trial. But it's important to see also that the experience we mean here, religious experience, is essentially not our experience of God, but rather God's experience of us. This occurs throughout our lives, as God tries and tests or 'experiences' us. Some of that experience, as we know, can come in the form of great suffering, which can certainly be profoundly distressing, even agonising, but the underlying, religious consolation of all such trials is that, to the eyes of faith, they are a sign that our lives are being touched and moulded by the grace of a merciful God, they are not just floating aimlessly and meaninglessly through time and space.

Yet it's curious how the expression, 'to be at someone's mercy', usually has quite an ominous meaning, whereas mercy is actually one of the names of God. The popular sense, however, of 'being at someone's mercy' shows perhaps an instinctive awareness that the mercy of God can have, from our perspective, a dark, even a harrowing side (hinted at also perhaps in the popular religious expression: 'if God spares us'). Perhaps it's a side God's mercy must have if it is to be ultimately beneficial for us. Now, why a good God allows suffering is the perennial question. But trust in the goodness of God who didn't deny or shirk the mystery of evil, but willed to absorb it into himself in the suffering and death of his incarnate Son, Jesus Christ – trust in the goodness of God and in the goodness of his will for us – has been the central message of Christianity down through the ages. As the greatest Christian poet of the Middle Ages, Dante, put it: 'And in His will is our peace.'[15]

The reference in today's gospel to 'wailing and grinding of teeth' is often interpreted as an allusion to the end of the world, to the Last Judgement. And this latter term too, like the notion of 'mercy', has frequently taken on ominous, frightening overtones in the course of Christian history. But, if we believe in the goodness of our hidden God, then the Last Judgement itself should surely be understood in terms of a gracious, ultimate revelation of God's mercy towards us, something we should be looking forward to rather than something we should be dreading. If the peace of God, as the New Testament claims, surpasses all understanding and can 'justify' the world with all its pain, then we should expect the hidden side of God's mercy to be able to surpass gloriously the suffering that seems to us now to be permanently inseparable from creation.

And that same peace might even finally enable us to suspend judgement here and hereafter about the rightness of God's ways in dealing with us – not in a spirit of resignation, but with a good conscience. For we are ultimately dealing here with a case we can never realistically bring to any court, as Job discovered. And this really, perhaps, is why the church has always insisted on the difference between faith and reason. We can trust in God's goodness and mercy, but we cannot define it or know it or judge it. And God surely wouldn't expect us to pass an affirmative judgement on something where the only one who has the right to do so is God himself.

God's Risk[16]

It is a sobering thought to realise that Jesus was put to death by representatives of the established order in both state and religion. He wasn't killed by people we normally think of as evil: he wasn't killed by gangsters or terrorists or criminals, but by people we normally think of as guardians of law and order.

From the religious point of view, what occurred was a clash between two different interpretations of scripture. Jesus saw his death as foretold in scripture. As he says in the gospel reading today: 'The Son of Man does indeed go to his fate even as it has been decreed … ', and later: 'Yes, what scripture says about me is even now reaching its fulfilment.' The leaders of his people, however, didn't recognise him as fulfilling their scriptures, but as contradicting them. It was this difference in understanding the scriptures that provoked the tragic clash between Jesus and the leaders of his own people, which climaxed in the death of Jesus and brought the human race to redemption.

If those who killed Jesus had been self-evidently evil, his death would be less puzzling, certainly less moving. It is the fact that he was killed by ordinary, average people, doing their best in a difficult, volatile situation that is so shocking, and so unnerving. Because while it is unrealistic for most people to recognise themselves in some flamboyant criminal, it is much easier and much more realistic to recognise ourselves in the ordinary, normal people we meet in the gospels who for the most part just try to muddle through life as best they can, without really understanding what the whole business is all about and without any thought of doing anything heroically good or anything spectacularly evil on the way. The leaders of the Jews were just like that: ordinary men, trying to guide their people through a tricky political period, hoping for the best, wanting to keep major trouble at bay. And they were genuinely convinced that Jesus deserved to die for blaspheming, for claiming to be the Son of God.

How many of *our* actions, which we honestly think we are carrying out in accordance with the will of God, are in fact contrary to that will?

The story of the Passion raises yet again for us the ultimate question of who God is and of how he acts in history.

Jesus saw his death foretold in scripture. Does this mean that those who handed him over to death had no choice? They were in fact God's choice, members of the chosen people. Would it have been better for them had God not singled them out for special status?

Such questions are impossible to answer, but they are serious ones. There is an undercurrent of danger, of evil and of tragedy running through the Passion story, an awareness of the closeness of religion to catastrophe and failure and destruction. Man is God's risk, and that risk sometimes has disastrous consequences.

Yet it is part of the mystery of God that we can never know from human history just what exactly God is like or what he will do to us and for us. 'No one has ever seen God,' as St John puts it. So we can't pass the Last Judgement, which is God's judgement, on anyone, including those who handed Jesus over to death.

The paradox of *their* situation is that they triggered off a series of events that led finally to the death of Jesus. But without that death our redemption would not have been achieved. Are we then, perhaps, in some obscure way in their debt? No one probably would want to go that far. But we should recognise in them fellow human beings whose tragic careers prefigure our own mistakes and failures and whose need of redemption is the same as ours.

Yet over and above the mistakes and failures and tragedies of human history is the peace of God that surpasses all understanding, and the mercy of God that can bring good out of any evil. God raised up Jesus from the dead. Why shouldn't we hope that he will also raise up those who handed Jesus over to death and all of us whose humanity is no different from theirs?

GOD OR TRINITY?[17]

Today is Trinity Sunday, the Sunday of the year when the church places specifically before us our belief in God as Father, Son, and Holy Spirit. Now, if we reflect on what our faith tells us about God we might well ask: 'What difference does it make if we just talk about God as God rather than about God who is the Blessed Trinity of Father, Son, and Holy Spirit? What does the Trinity tell us about God that the word "God" itself doesn't tell us or can't tell us?' Christian faith says that we can get some kind of answer to that question if we look at Jesus Christ and try to understand the meaning of his life, death, and resurrection. In Jesus Christ, our faith claims, God revealed himself to us as our saviour.

Now, if God revealed himself to us or communicated with us through a human being, then that means that what God is like can best be conveyed to us in a human being, rather than, say, through a mighty event in nature. Very often when a natural catastrophe occurs, like an earthquake, or a hurricane, or an avalanche, you hear people say, 'It's the hand of God'. But Christianity, although it recognises God to be the creator of the world and to be in charge of all the forces of nature, doesn't say that God reveals himself or shows his hand supremely in those natural forces. No, our faith tells us that God showed his hand most truly and most unmistakably in Jesus Christ, who lived, died and was raised from the dead, so that the world might know God and have access to God. For, what was of greatest importance to Jesus was his relation to God his Father in prayer, and his relations with the people around him, the two being inseparable. As the New Testament puts it: 'How can you love the God you don't see, if you don't love the people around you that you do see?' Jesus loved those around him and wanted to lead them to God.

The God we seek, in other words, the God who was made man in Jesus Christ, is a God who chose to open up his life to share it with us, his creation. He didn't decide to live a kind of solo existence, but wanted to share his life with his creatures. We speak of God as being a living God. That must mean that there is a life within God, that God contains a living community within himself, which our predecessors in the faith came to understand as Father, Son, and Holy Spirit, an understanding they passed on to us. It was this divine life that God wanted to share with us in sending his Son into the world. And that in turn would seem to mean that we will only be at home with this God to the extent that we too open up our lives and share them with others.

But that of course is only one side of the story. The strange thing about Jesus Christ – and hence about God – is that no matter how much he shared his life with others and finally gave his life for others, he always remained elusive, mysterious and enigmatic and in so doing reflected accurately the impenetrable mystery of God we pray to as the Blessed Trinity. And we too, as God's creatures, made in his image and likeness, share to some extent in the hiddenness of God, and so we should respect that divine-like inaccessibility and unfathomability, that untouchability or 'inexposability', in ourselves and in others. That's to say, we shouldn't confuse openness and sharing with possessiveness or intrusiveness, just as in worshipping the Blessed Trinity we can give thanks and praise to God for opening up his life to us, but also acknowledge at the same time with awe and wonder that that divine life, which sustains and supports and enriches us, will always outreach and surprise us, and will always remain mysterious and unfathomable to us and for us, now and for ever.

THE DISCOVERY OF GOD[18]

St Patrick, as nearly everyone knows, is credited with being the person most responsible for bringing Christianity to Ireland. For that reason he is celebrated as the national Saint or almost as the national Apostle of Ireland. Apparently, though, Patrick was not the first Christian to reach Ireland. When he first came, or rather was forcibly brought, to Ireland, he discovered that there were already traces of the Christian faith to be found in the country. Christianity appears to have initially reached Ireland in a rather unorganised, even haphazard way through traders, who may have travelled to Ireland from Spain. Or it may even have been brought by monks, who left their own homelands – Egypt or Syria, it has been suggested – on the shores of the eastern Mediterranean in order to seek God in the wilderness of a distant foreign land like Ireland, at the end of the then known world, and as far away as possible from its corruption and compromises. Patrick, however, is credited with being the one who, it seems safe to say, was the first to put some kind of shape on the organisation of the Christian church in Ireland.

Yet to see St Patrick simply as the bringer of the Christian gospel to Ireland, or even to see him as the first important organiser of church life in Ireland, is not to see the full picture of his life, or even perhaps the most important aspect of his life. Sometimes, indeed, seeing St Patrick exclusively as the most important of the Christian missionaries to come to Ireland can turn him into a one-dimensional character or plaster saint whose life ran like clockwork, guided smoothly and infallibly by the hand of God. To see St Patrick in this way is to ignore something of great importance about him. For Patrick wasn't always a missionary; he wasn't, if you like, a born Christian missionary.

The young Patrick grew up in what was then the Roman province of Britain, in a fairly privileged environment: his father held prominent positions in, as we might now say, both church and state. Although baptised and raised as a Christian, Patrick apparently did not take his religion too seriously in his early years. Being a Christian would, in those days, have been the normal, socially acceptable, unexceptional thing to be in his society. It was only when the young Patrick was kidnapped and brought to Ireland and had to work as a shepherd in the north of Ireland, thus losing the privileged conditions of his early years, that he began to take his life and the meaning or direction of his life more seriously. It was only then that his Christian faith became *real* for him, we might say, so that, after finally escaping from captivity in Ireland, he eventually decided to return freely to Ireland as a missionary.

A lesson that might be drawn from Patrick's life is that God can bring unimaginable, incalculable good out of evil, not just for the person to whom evil was done (in this case, Patrick himself), but to those who benefited, and continue to benefit right down to the present day, from his response to the situation of evil that was inflicted upon him.

On the other hand, there are those who would argue, in the light of Ireland's wars of religion, that it might have been better had Patrick chosen another land for his missionary endeavours. But such historical 'might-have-beens' are perhaps doubly irrelevant to Patrick's story. In the first place, history can never be undone. And, second, and more importantly, to repeat the principal truth of Patrick's life, Christianity is a religion that does not deny the reality – and perhaps, inevitability[19] – of evil; it claims, however, that God cannot be defeated by evil, and indeed can even be relied on to bring unexpected good out of evil. This is at least part of what is meant by describing Christianity as a religion not primarily of enlightenment, but of redemption. St Patrick's life and destiny bear witness to the plausibility of that description.

PRAYER[20]

Today's gospel takes up a theme that could be regarded as the very essence of the religious life, and that is of course the theme of prayer. It's a theme that runs through all the gospels, and right down to our own day it has remained a vitally important aspect of Christian faith, if not its very life blood. And the great joys and sadnesses of life, which figure so much in the life of prayer, haven't changed very much either over the course of time.

It is no secret, however, that many people have always had great difficulties with prayer, and they still do. And this is so because we often don't know exactly how we should pray. Or rather, prayer presents us with huge difficulties because we perhaps inwardly suspect or fear that, despite all our praying, we won't ever get any answer from God.

Jesus seems to take account of such fears and suspicions in today's gospel in the parable he tells about the unjust judge. In this parable, Jesus faces up to the great question of seemingly unheard prayers when he describes how a very harsh, even slightly cynical judge deals with the burning demand for justice made of him by an apparently defenceless, and for the judge, troublesome and tiresome widow. But in the parable, Jesus recounts how even an unjust judge finally did decide to deal with the widow's case – not from any noble concern for justice or from any high-minded desire to come to the aid of the weakest and most vulnerable in society, but simply to get the widow out of his hair. In telling this parable, Jesus seems to be trying to encourage his listeners and raise their spirits by suggesting to them that even if a bit of a scoundrel of a judge will deliver the goods to a poor widow, how much more willingly and effectively will God come to our rescue and to our help when we pray to him. Indeed, the implication of Jesus' words is that God can be relied on to be far more effective in helping us than the unjust judge was, who finally did in fact help the widow in question.

However, consoling though such an idea undoubtedly is, it doesn't really answer the question we began with of how we should pray and what we can expect from God if we do pray, or even if we can expect any answer at all from God to our prayers. Even today's gospel seems to admit that there is no easy answer to such questions, because this gospel reading ends with the question: 'But when the Son of Man comes, will he find any faith on earth?' If prayer were really all that simple and all that unproblematic, it presumably wouldn't have been necessary to raise this question at all. However, the fact that this question is in the gospel is surely a consolation for us because it shows that both Jesus and the evangelist, Luke, who relates Jesus' words to us in his gospel, both knew how difficult prayer is, and indeed not just prayer, but the reality out of which all prayer grows, namely life itself on this earth. Life is littered with so many reverses and devastating blows of various kinds that affect people so deeply and so powerfully that they are often scarcely able to know how they can continue to go on living, let alone continue to pray.

But, on the other hand, it has also been said – strange though it may sound – that prayers should never be answered, because, if they were, then prayer could become or could degenerate into a kind of correspondence (Oscar Wilde). That is of course a very drastic way of making a point, the point being that God isn't at our disposal, and doesn't stand in the same relationship to us as other people do. We can't conduct a correspondence with God the way we might do with other people. For, if we could, then God wouldn't in fact be God any more. God's frequent silence in our lives is the high price that we have to pay if we want to believe in the true God and not in a god we create in the image of ourselves and our own needs, a god who would always do whatever we asked him or told him to do.

On the other hand, however, the famous Cistercian monk, St Bernard of Clairvaux, also once said that only God is never sought in vain, even when we can't find him.[21] The fact that God often is or often seems to be silent in our lives doesn't mean that he's not there, but only that he isn't doing what we maybe want him to do in our lives at any particular moment. Our faith means and demands, if it is genuine, that we have to leave it up to God to decide what is really good for us, or, as today's gospel puts it, how God is to see justice done to us. We ourselves often don't know what is best for ourselves, for the simple reason that we don't know everything and can't take everything into account and evaluate it. And there may be other reasons that are even more hidden from us why we don't – or can't – know what is best for us. We can undoubtedly rule certain things out where God is concerned, but it is much more difficult to know what to rule in. We can believe, for instance, that, while God may be complicated, he's not malicious. And, on the affirmative side, we can rule in that God is good and wills the best for us. That's why we pray in the Our Father, in the prayer that Jesus gave us, not primarily, or first and foremost, for ourselves and our own needs, but we pray that God's name may be 'hallowed' or 'made holy' and that his kingdom may come. But knowledge of why all this is so seems to lie outside the range of human reason, and to belong to the dark night of faith, which in Christian experience would appear to be a necessary prerequisite for the enjoyment of the full glory of God's kingdom.

The faith that lies behind the Our Father did in fact help our predecessors to go on living and to go on passing on life, together with their faith in God, to their descendants. Otherwise, we wouldn't be here today. In this mass we can pray that this same faith in God will help us get through what is frequently the desert of life and allow us to hand on this life-giving and life-enduring faith to those who come after us.

GRACE AND
REDEMPTION

The Scandal of Christianity[1]

The question of whether Christianity is a blessing or a curse was raised by journalist and broadcaster Vincent Browne in an article for the *Sunday Business Post* of 18 March 2007. While this issue was raised specifically in relation to St Patrick and Ireland, it clearly has wider ramifications, which are not of today or yesterday, but go back almost to the birth of Christianity. The idea that there is something scandalous and foolish or even absurd about Christianity has shadowed it from its beginnings. It's what it says about itself, as St Paul's contribution to the New Testament amply testifies. And some, like the early Christian writer Tertullian, have famously and defiantly gloried in its absurdity. The most celebrated recent trickster in this regard is Søren Kierkegaard in the nineteenth century.

But something even more sinister than absurdity has also been associated with Christianity, and this is perhaps the nub of the matter, as far as Vincent Browne is concerned and those who think as he does. This is the idea, which has provoked intense hostility towards the Christian faith from Julian the Apostate to Friedrich Nietzsche, that Christianity is anti-human. Not just with its otherworldliness, which appears to undervalue the significance and beauty of this world. Not just with its sometimes less than intellectually honest or convincing theology ('There is really nothing more compromising for God than his theologians', as Franz Overbeck wrote[2]). Not just with its Augustinian, potentially demoralising sense of human sinfulness and corruption, which seems to undermine any human effort at improving the world from the outset, and not just because of its corresponding teaching about the human need for a divine redeemer.

Rather, Christianity has been found abhorrent, above all, because of the way the act of redemption – Christ's death on the cross – has been understood. The idea that, in Vincent Browne's words, 'an all-merciful, all-loving and all-forgiving God was so obsessed with the sinfulness of humanity, that to atone to Himself for that sinfulness, He sent His Son into the world to be tortured and crucified to save us all from His (God's) wrath' is indeed repulsive and incredible. Such a sadistic God, who enjoyed torturing his own Son and who by implication enjoys tormenting the inhabitants of a world he has created for no other apparent reason, would, if he existed, be a monster. One might conceivably have to acknowledge his existence, but one would have to loathe such a deity. Or, more likely, admit sardonically, with Stendhal, that 'God's only excuse is that he does not exist'.[3]

So far, the caricature. But even if it is conceded that Vincent Browne presents only a caricature of Christian beliefs, it is worth remembering that a caricature only exaggerates or distorts for emphasis something that is essentially true. Christianity does indeed interpret the death of Christ on the cross as effecting the redemption of the world. The sacrifice of the mass celebrates this belief. There is no getting round this or rendering it less unpalatable or less offensive to human reason. As Vincent Browne writes:

> At the heart of Christianity is the symbol and story of the crucifixion. The cross is the ubiquitous symbol of the Catholic faith – and yet the story of the cross is not just literally incredible, but also disturbing.

Even if one tries to 'soften' the impact of the crucifixion by appealing to the resurrection, the scandal still remains. Resurrection, in a sense, 'proves' nothing, or justifies nothing because it doesn't undo the past and its sufferings. Even St Paul's teaching that 'the sufferings of this present time are not worthy to be compared with the glory which shall be revealed in us' (Rom 8:18), many have found to be unacceptable in any straightforward or obvious sense. Even if given its most benign interpretation – that it was propounded by Paul in the context of his belief in the relative shortness of 'this present time' and a correspondingly acute conviction about the imminence of the second coming of Christ – Paul's teaching has been called into question on the ground that any gratuitous suffering inflicted on human beings (or any other species) is incompatible with belief in an all-powerful and benevolent God. This, presumably, is Ivan's point in Dostoevsky's *The Brothers Karamazov* when he argues that the price of redemption is too high, so that even if a God who offered heaven to all his followers existed, and even if torturers and victims were to be reconciled in such a heaven, he, Ivan, would not accept his entry ticket. The price to be paid in terms of human suffering is simply too high, too unjustifiably high. And examples of a similar outlook could be multiplied, especially after the events of the last century. The eloquent testimony of Auschwitz survivor, Primo Levi, can stand for what many concluded after the Holocaust:

> Like [Jean] Améry, I too entered the Lager as a non-believer, and as a non-believer I was liberated and have lived to this day; actually, the experience of the Lager with its frightful iniquity has confirmed me in my laity. It has prevented me, and still prevents me, from conceiving of any form of providence or transcendent justice.[4]

This perhaps brings us closer to what Christianity, I think, 'means' by the crucifixion. It has nothing to do with smoothing the ruffled feathers of an easily offended, testy deity; nor has it anything to do with a 'neurotic' God 'obsessed with the sinfulness of humanity', or feeling miffed that he was being ignored by his ungrateful creatures. But it has everything to do with our acceptance of life and death, with whether we are willing to endure the sufferings of life, including seemingly inevitable injustices and certainly inevitable death, for the benefit of existing, rather than condemn life, as the Gnostics – early Christianity's most incisive adversaries – were wont to do, as an irremediable disaster. As interpreted by Christianity, Jesus, with his 'ignominious death' on the cross, was, in the words of Leszek Kolakowski, 'to become not only the most powerful symbol in religious history but a symbol whereby man gained a penetrating insight into his own destiny'.[5] For, so much of human history is characterised by suffering, defeat and death that the figure of the crucified Christ has been for many a uniquely poignant reflection of the absurdity and horror and wastefulness of their own lives. But yet the miracle of Christianity is that no amount of ignominy and humiliation and suffering has in fact been able to extinguish faith in the value of our humanity, as reflected – or rather as incarnated – in the figure of Jesus. It has, rather, emphasised that value.

Nietzsche, Christianity's most passionately serious critic in the modern age, saw too the problem of suffering in life with finally unbearable lucidity. To live and to realise how living is inseparable from suffering (both the suffering we cause and the suffering we endure), to recognise how suffering cannot be 'edited out' of the texture of life, is to see that a 'price' has to be paid for living. The question then is, 'Who picks up the tab?' or, in more traditional language, 'Who pays the price of our redemption?' Who can 'redeem' life and make it liveable and worthwhile? It is, with respect, more than a question of morality, or more than what Vincent Browne seems to have in mind, when he writes: 'The only sensible (I believe) concept of sinfulness has to do essentially with justice – or rather injustice – or with the unfair treatment of others.' Morality is, of course, important, but ultimate questions are about more than morality. They are, in Nietzsche's expression, 'Beyond Good and Evil'. Is life to be endorsed or repudiated? Should the human race have a future? Is the game worth the candle?

Nietzsche, and those heroic figures, like Yeats, who 'cast out remorse' and endorse the deep course of things ('To redeem the past and to transform every "It was" into an "I wanted it thus!" – that alone do I call redemption!'),[6] would answer and do answer 'Yes' emphatically to all ultimate questions about the value of existence. Life, despite all its horrors, is worth living, and should never be rejected or denied. Nietzsche concentrated his own repudiation of Christianity in his preference for Dionysus (the Greek god of wine, who is associated with excess and destruction) over Christ (the 'Crucified One'), as if to take upon himself and arrogate to himself the justification of existence, as if to bring his own being and the meaning or value of life together, to overcome the gulf between the two.

Overcoming a gulf is, I think, what is really involved in Christian talk about sin and redemption. 'Sin' is, at bottom, not about contravening divine, and possibly arbitrary, injunctions, but about 'separation' or 'sundering' (the two words 'sin' and 'sunder' may be cognate): the sundering of human beings from 'meaning' or 'value' or – dare one say it? – 'God'.

Christianity, as I understand it, takes the view that, because of our contingency (i.e. we did not create the world or ourselves), we do not have the wherewithal to make such a claim as Nietzsche makes about the meaning or value of life, but can only endorse the value of life by faith, that is to say, by believing that God in Christ took upon himself the evil and suffering of life and thereby 'redeemed' life. He did so, however, not out of a sadistic, or masochistic, love of suffering, but out of a desire to let the world exist, despite its woes. From our perspective – and what other have we? – it really depends on how we view 'life' and its ultimate origin and end.

If God is suppressed from consideration, can we talk about justice or injustice at all, in other than a pragmatic sense? If there is no God, we cannot be made in his image. So in what or in whose image are we made? What is our meaning? What is our value? What is our identity? And if we do believe in God, but believe that God did not create the world out of any inner divine necessity or out of any self-seeking motive (which is what the doctrine of creation out of nothing — *creatio ex nihilo* — surely implies), is God then wilfully responsible for the suffering of the world? Is he, in that case, an irresponsible God? Would it not have been better had nothing ever existed?

The Christian faith with, as Vincent Browne rightly recognises, the reality of the crucified Christ at its centre is at heart an attempt to answer that question of all questions. And hence, perhaps Christian faith, as it has always traditionally insisted, even if sometimes clumsily, has a lot more to do with the acceptance of suffering for the sake of life (created by God), and hence for God's sake, rather than with the correct intellectual expression of this attitude. Important though thought – or theology – undeniably is and for Christian faith, as long as this world lasts, always will be, Christianity, while by no means surrendering to irrationality, is finally more about confronting the existential than the rational challenges of reality. And maybe this is what some theologians mean when they talk about theology needing to be 'pastoral', though it would be an odd interpretation of theology that would ever have seen it as anything else.

Those who were possibly upset by Vincent Browne's views, as he generously conceded at the start of his article that they might be, should rather be grateful to him for pinpointing so unerringly what is the real nature of the Christian religious question.

The Weakness and Strength of Christianity[7]

That divine and human wisdom do not necessarily coincide is an ancient idea whose validity, in the Christian world at any rate, may not depend solely on the rhetorical talent of its first proponent, St Paul. Similarly, the reversal of apparently self-evident ideas – for example, that strength is superior to weakness, or that fame is preferable to obscurity – has not just been part of the stock-in-trade of Christian apologetics over the centuries, but seems to be woven into the fundamental experience of humanity. 'Greatness' comes eventually to be revealed as megalomania, and 'fame', as the Chinese sage Chuang Tzu, has it, 'is the beginning of disgrace'.

In Christianity, the symbol of crucifixion is held to embody the paradox of 'strength in weakness' in so unsurpassable a form that it is, perhaps for that very reason, also taken to reveal the most incontrovertible and inescapable truth about the human condition, characterised as it is by contingency or uncontrollability. Human passivity in the endurance of suffering and death – life's two constants – is concentrated unforgettably in the image of a public crucifixion, but so also is the refusal to shirk the misfortunes of reality, without which life is unimaginable. It is as if existence without pain were a contradiction in terms, and as if faith in the value of existence were not open to negotiation, because nothing could ever be strong enough or awful enough to undermine it: so, the universal language of the cross.

So far, so good. Yet the fact that something cannot be undermined does not necessarily make it true. That must be granted. But, on the other hand, to want to know what the 'positive' truth of Christian faith consists in, to want to know why, for example, there is good and evil in the world, or to want to know what, for example, 'resurrection' means would be like wanting to have absolute control of life, or in more traditional language, it would be like wanting to 'be like God', or again, to use the images already evoked, it would be like wanting to transcend the limits of evil and suffering and death that the cross simplifies, intensifies and clarifies for us. It cannot be done. And any claim that it had been done must be fraudulent. Not that humanity's appetite for such hidden knowledge ever wanes, but attempts to satisfy it are always lethal. Hence it is probably good that the positive truth of Christianity can only be seen with the eyes of faith, but can never be known. The weakness of Christianity – that no one knows what it means – is therefore, once again, its strength, and so the snide remark, attributed to Lenin, that 'theology is a subject without an object' is not – at least as far as Christianity is concerned – a jibe to be anxiously refuted, but an unwitting revelation of the truth.

THE POWER OF ANGELS[8]

The Annunciation scene in the New Testament (Lk 1:26-38) is one of the better-known parts of the gospels, its popularity owing much, no doubt, to its incorporation in the centuries-old devotion of the Angelus. But even many of those who have little or no attachment to Catholic Christianity are familiar with the Annunciation because it has been so frequently represented in the history of western art. Its fascination for artists suggests that from this simple scene a message emerges that transcends the framework of historical Christianity in which it was first formulated, and addresses some more general or fundamental truth about the human situation. And yet, this scene has a very precise and definite origin that lies in the first stirrings of Christianity.

In order to approach these early beginnings even tentatively, one might bear in mind that the scene of the Annunciation can probably only be rightly understood if viewed against the background of the meaning that angels had in Jewish culture and literature in, roughly, the two centuries before the birth of Jesus. For, at that time, the myth of the 'fall of the angels' was very much alive in Judaism and was even appealed to, much more than the 'fall' of Adam and Eve, to explain the source of evil in the world.[9] In this context the term 'angel' had by no means the almost entirely positive resonance it has for us today. The myth of the fall of the angels can already be found adumbrated in the Book of Genesis, where we read about 'the sons of God' – later understood as 'angels' – marrying 'the daughters of men' (Gen 6:2). The offspring of such unions were known as the 'Nephilim' (Gen 6:4), a term that seems to have originally meant 'the fallen ones'[10] – 'mighty men ... of old, the men of renown' (Gen 6:4), giants who were warriors and famous heroes, but whose actions brought catastrophe upon the human race and finally provoked, as divine retribution, the biblical flood described in Genesis.

In the few centuries before the birth of Jesus, such ambiguous and threatening 'angelic' figures were to be identified, in the imaginative Jewish apocalyptic literature of the period, with the new military and cultural power in the Jewish world, the successors of Alexander the Great, and, somewhat later still, with the Romans, who replaced the former Hellenistic rulers. Such world powers made their presence felt within Judaism above all by their military might, behaving as if they were gods or sons of gods ('angels'), in their own eyes at least, and being happy to be fêted as such. As tends to be the case with occupying armies, the attitude they adopted to the women of the weaker peoples they had conquered was not marked by any excessive reticence. Those of Jewish origin who first heard the gospel preached will undoubtedly have had this specific historical background in mind, and will have been aware of the sinister, ambiguous aura surrounding the figure of an 'angel', whereas for us today such natural awareness of the cultural background, not just to the Annunciation scene, but to so many aspects of the gospel story, is clearly no longer automatic.

Nevertheless, we can at least try by an effort of the imagination to put ourselves in the place of the earliest Christians, who came mainly from the world of Judaism. And if we are willing to do so, it should not be too difficult to sense an element of surprise and reversal of expectations in the fact that the angel who approached Mary in the Annunciation scene was anything but an overbearing or menacing force seeking possibly to exploit her,[11] but was rather a force for good, wishing only to transmit a divine message. And the birth of the child ('the Son of God') that is announced is also quite different from the birth of, say, a violent, militarily powerful ruler, destined to conquer the world. And neither is Mary herself, despite her connection with the house of David through Joseph that Luke also mentions, an important personality in any worldly sense. She has no association with any ruling élite, but is rather a woman of the people. But despite this, the angel does also use the language of power in delivering his message, when he announces that the son Mary will bear will rule over the house of Jacob for ever and that his kingdom will have no end.

The question is, of course, what kind of power and rule is meant here. It seems clear, in the first instance, that no traditional, worldly understanding of power and rule is involved. For the contrast with purely worldly power is highlighted in the Annunciation scene by the fact that not even in the birth of the child is any human effort said to be involved in the realisation of what is announced, but only the power of God. In short, God is said to be active in bringing about a different kind of reality from that which purely human power can achieve in this world. And hence Mary's passive response to the angel: 'Behold, I am the handmaid of the Lord; let it be done to me according to your word.'

The Annunciation scene expresses the redeeming difference that exists between the reality of God and the reality of all exclusively human power, which so often degenerates into cruelty and catastrophe. For the reality of God is other than that of the world, and, even more significantly, it cannot be undermined or ultimately held in check by any inner-worldly force. This simple but revolutionary truth, which suffuses the entire Bible, is articulated in one way among many others in the New Testament by the inclusion of the Annunciation scene in the gospel of Luke, who is in fact the only evangelist to describe it. The scene's attraction for future generations may have its source in the other-worldly atmosphere that surrounds it, but it remains for all that – or rather, perhaps, because of that – an enduring question mark over our understanding of this-worldly power.

THE CONSOLATIONS OF DARKNESS[12]

It is slightly ironic that the Son of God, the light of the world, should have been born not during the hours of daylight, but in the middle of the night. This was a feature of Christ's birth that was often commented upon in the early church. From earliest times, Christian thinkers saw a profound significance in the fact that Christ was born at night, and not in the daytime. They saw a deep symbolical meaning in the circumstances of Christ's birth. The natural light of our world is, of course, the sun, which shines by day and clarifies our world for us, thereby, however, also concealing by its own light the marvels of the starry sky.

So, in calling Christ, who was born during the hours of darkness, the light of the world, the early Christians believed that, with Christ, they were dealing with something other than the natural light of the sun. They believed that with the birth of Christ a light had come into their world that was of a different quality from the natural light of the sun. The source of the light Christ brought, the source of the light he incarnated, was not thought of as natural, but supernatural. It was a light that came directly from God. It was not the created light of the sun, but the saving light of God himself; not, fundamentally, the light of creation, but the light of redemption.

However, there was a further significance the early Christians saw in the fact that Christ came into the world during the night. They knew that night is also a symbol of the frequent darkness of human history. And in seeing Christ's light as illuminating the darkness, they believed that the light of Christ was a force that none of the darkness of this world could ever overcome, as St John was to put it in the opening chapter of his gospel. It was this faith or conviction that the first Christians passed on to subsequent generations, and it is still the same faith that continues to justify the unique place Christmas – the season of goodwill – still holds in our culture. For why exercise goodwill in a world ruled and controlled ultimately and irredeemably by ill will and malice? It is, in other words, the belief that, no matter how terrible or awful human history may be or become, it can never overpower or extinguish the light of Christ, it is this belief that gives the Christmas season its most credible, theological *raison d'être*.

But it must be conceded that this is a belief or a claim, the Good News, indeed, that Christianity has to tell; it is not a statement of scientific fact. Facts consist of things like our awareness of the grim truth that even at this moment, while it is fairly peaceful here and now in this particular part of our planet, elsewhere in our world the darkness of life is also a reality in the wars, destruction, terror and crime that have always constituted the murky shadow-side of human history. Christianity has, however, always been inspired by the belief that Christ's redemptive and saving light will until the end of time be more powerful than any human darkness, because it is, to the eyes of faith, a light that is not of a natural, but a supernatural, indeed a divine origin, and God cannot finally be defeated by any force from within his own creation. But this is, to repeat the point, a belief or a claim; it is not a statement of fact.

It must also be conceded that this simple, but profound Christian faith, which came into the world roughly 2,000 years ago, has not driven away all the shadows of our world, but it has continued to shine throughout the past two millennia and it can continue to illuminate our path through the 'night of the world', as St Augustine once put it, and lead us into the full daylight of God's kingdom in heaven. The good news of Christmas that doesn't age or change is that the Son of God who became incarnate for us on the first Christmas night almost 2,000 years ago is also God's promise that humanity's long journey through the night of history will not have been in vain but will finally be seen to have been justified.[13] However, no amount of ecclesiastical urging or theological huffing and puffing can give this faith any higher status than that of a claim, whose credibility resides, as far as the naked eye can judge, at least penultimately in the lives of those who profess it. But for those who believe in the triumphant reality of goodness, this should be more than enough.

GRACE AND WORKS

In a short piece called 'Acts and Grace,'[14] the Polish writer Czeslaw Milosz draws attention to the fact that in the Middle Ages, when people supposedly had a strong faith in God, those same people sinned as enthusiastically as those in more modern times, when religious faith has allegedly receded. Milosz wonders whether some insight into this strange state of affairs might not have made Luther opt for sheer grace over works in the question of human salvation. In a somewhat similar way, Nietzsche had a keen sense of life's unbudging parameters. Along with Christianity, with which he was otherwise in conflict, and indeed Schopenhauer, whose influence he also in time outgrew, he accepted that the fundamental features of human life, the essentials of the human condition, always remain the same ('that eternal basic text, *homo natura*'[15]). Consequently, he acknowledged, at an early date, that living in the world was inseparable from acquiescing in its injustice.[16] This awareness eventually led him to give a blanket endorsement to all reality as the only way in which life could be honestly lived.

Nietzsche, of course, doesn't speak of *sola gratia*, or of the transcendent importance of grace over good works in the matter of human salvation, but he speaks instead of affirming the reality of the world in all its moods and tenses. This heroic gesture, which appealed to Yeats (who echoes it in his own poetry, e.g. 'A Dialogue of Self and Soul', 'Lapis Lazuli'), seeks to be redemptive,[17] though Nietzsche's sceptical, clear-eyed friend, Franz Overbeck, characterised the former's heroic affirmation of the world as the 'optimism ... of a desperado'.[18]

Assuming, however, that life is in fact unjust and, in its vital ingredients, immutable, irreformable, what attitude can or should one adopt towards it? Christianity proposes redemption by the grace of God, Nietzsche the total affirmation of life. Yet is Nietzsche's 'yea-saying' perhaps an involuntary echo of the 'God saw that it was good' of Genesis? Nietzsche appears to be implying that it is impossible to believe in God without believing that one is oneself divine, and equally impossible to believe in redemption without being oneself the author of that redemption.

UNDERSTANDING OR SALVATION?

In his celebrated book, *El Laberinto de la Soledad* (*The Labyrinth of Solitude*), the Mexican writer Octavio Paz discusses at one point the career of the seventeenth-century Hieronymite Mexican nun, Sor Juana Inés de la Cruz, and argues that she perceived the world as a problem or an enigma, rather than a place where a drama of salvation or perdition was being played out.[19] This, in Paz's view, reveals Sor Juana, quite exceptionally for someone of her time and condition, to be more an intellectual truth-seeker than a religious apologist. To that extent, he claims, she is a modern figure, committed to the search for disinterested, intellectual truth, not, by implication, tied first and foremost to the defence of an inherited religious system.

Be that as it may, a question one might raise in this context is whether there is an irreconcilable conflict, not simply between faith and reason, whose relationship so often resembles that of an uneasy truce between two mutually suspicious rivals, but, perhaps more interestingly, between what might be called a 'religious' temperament and an 'intellectual' one. That is to say, do some regard the world, instinctively and primarily, as needing to be redeemed, while others, equally instinctively and primarily, regard it as needing to be understood? And do these alternatives reflect an irreconcilable difference between two fundamental human stances *vis-à-vis* the world? Or can one have it both ways, so to speak, desiring to understand the world while longing for its redemption? And where, if anywhere, does Christianity stand on this question? Is Christianity, in other words, principally a religion promising illumination and understanding of the world, or a religion offering the world redemption, or is it perhaps both?

Historically, at any rate, the answer would seem to be clear. Christianity has spawned so much theology down the centuries, even defining theology, with St Anselm, as 'faith seeking understanding', that, apart from the commitment to preaching the Good News of Salvation, there would also appear to be no doubt about Christianity's commitment to the business of understanding, if not the world, at least itself – even at the risk of getting perilously close to Gnosticism (identifying salvation with knowledge) in the process. And surely Christianity can scarcely seek to understand itself without trying at the same time to understand the world that God is believed to have created.

And yet, the doubts remain, doubts about how Christianity really gauges its priorities and allegiances. As Christianity has not only encouraged faith to seek understanding, but has also been vigilant, not to say violent, in rooting out interpretations of the faith considered erroneous or heretical, some might argue that this shows how serious Christianity's commitment to intellectual truth is, while others might judge such an argument disingenuous. For, to resort to violence in support of an intellectual commitment is surely to betray and undermine it. And this reveals, even if somewhat perversely, that Christianity's chief commitment can scarcely be to intellectual truth *per se*. Christianity's overriding concern is with redemption, even though this concern may sometimes have taken on bizarre forms, as the evidence of heresy-hunting sadly reveals.

Furthermore, doubts about whether Christianity's uppermost concern can really be with understanding are nourished by none other than St Paul himself, despite the fact that he was the first thinker to try to systematise the beliefs of the new Christian faith. For though St Paul did seek to interpret Christianity intellectually, he also allowed himself an escape hatch from too much understanding by playing off dramatically the foolishness of God against the wisdom of man and by claiming, defiantly, that Christianity offers a peace beyond understanding.

But the enduring dialectic between faith and reason that has been an undeniable feature of Christianity since the time of St Paul reinforces the notion that understanding is still more likely to be regarded as a valid aspect of redemption, rather than its utter antithesis. For Christian faith, redemption can truly be experienced, if only fleetingly, in the realm of the mind. It can be experienced, if only partially, in the relief that comes from discerning an intellectual order ('something understood', in George Herbert's understated phrase), where hitherto there had been only the chaotic obscurity of life.

Yet support for the conjecture that understanding can only ever be a fairly fragile aspect of redemption comes not just from the negative evidence supplied by the fate that so often befalls heterodoxy's perceived misinterpretations of Christianity. It comes also, and ultimately perhaps more persuasively, from the magnificent failures of the human mind's attempts to comprehend reality by the power of thought, not least in the case of Sor Juana herself in her *Primero sueño*. As Arthur Terry has written: '[Sor Juana's] masterpiece is the *Primero sueño*, a dream vision of the universe which dramatises the failure of the human mind to grasp reality by intellectual means.'[20]

While it would undoubtedly be in poor taste to hail the failures of reason as triumphs of faith, such failures do demonstrate that we are not pure spirits. Solving life's enigmas, however alleviating or invigorating for our minds, can scarcely constitute the fulfilment of all our needs. Human salvation, in other words, whatever it may ultimately consist in, cannot be expressed in terms of pure thought alone. It is, rather, the reality, constituting the redemptive heart of the Christian faith, to which the martyrs bore witness. It is the reality that, 'made all Platonic tolerance vain/And vain all Doric discipline,'[21] in Yeat's lapidary assertion. It cannot be stated at all, but only 'stammered' at, as St John of the Cross suggests in one of his most arresting and almost miraculously onomatopoeic lines: *'Un no sé qué que quedan balbuciendo.'*[22]

The Kabbalah, Paul Celan and a View of Redemption[23]

The Kabbalah (literally, 'received' or 'tradition') is a mystical, esoteric form of Judaism which flourished especially in southern France and Spain in the twelfth and thirteenth centuries. Like so many forms of Judaism, it has also been influential on Christianity, and was studied by, among others, the Renaissance philosopher Pico della Mirandola and the German humanist Johannes Reuchlin.

The Kabbalah contains speculations about the nature of God and the relationship between God and the universe. Both its view of creation (resulting not from the overflowing of God's goodness, but from an act of divine self-limitation that permits the world to emerge) and its view of redemption ('the Kabbalah ... made the salvation of God by man, the *tikkun*, as vital a matter as its contrary'[24]), are at first sight startling doctrines.

The unconventional notion of redemption as applying to God, rather than man, can also be found in Paul Celan's poem, 'Tenebrae'. To what extent, if at all, Celan may have been influenced by the Kabbalah is unknown to me, but he 'was very familiar with Jewish tradition and was an ardent reader of Gershom Scholem's studies on Jewish mysticism'.[25] Michael Hamburger observes that 'Celan is known to have been well versed in both [Jewish and Christian mysticism]'.[26] Celan's poem, hovering between a tormented mockery of the traditional religious understanding of redemption, and a harrowing awareness of a newly discovered religious no man's land, is, like all his poetry, written in reaction to the murderous enactment by the Third Reich of the kind of volatile political messianism that was, ironically, so powerful in certain Jewish circles a few centuries earlier as 'Sabbatianism',[27] a movement itself influenced by kabbalistic ideas.

That such shocking ideas on redemption, as one finds in kabbalistic writings or in Celan's 'Tenebrae', were even thinkable is an indication of not just how intractable – and yet how resilient – the challenge of evil to belief in God actually is, but also how any account, no matter how disturbing, of the reality of evil and suffering seems to be preferable to no account at all. Even more so they show how even the suggestion that there might be a 'point' to evil and suffering seems to some to be not too high a price to pay for saving the idea of 'God'.

Is there Anything Higher than the Forgiveness of Sins?[28]

'The special feature of Easter,' Pope Leo the Great said, 'is that it is the occasion when the whole church rejoices over the forgiveness of sins.' All the readings for today, the third Sunday of Easter, also point in various ways to sin and its forgiveness as central to Christianity. And 'the forgiveness of sins', one might add, is the only sacrament to be mentioned in the Apostles' Creed.

The Apostles' Creed was, of course, formulated a long time ago. With the passage of time, the intimate connection that the early church perceived between Christ's suffering and resurrection and the forgiveness of sins seems to have faded somewhat. When we nowadays celebrate the resurrection in the Easter season, what tends to be uppermost in our minds, it seems to me, is the belief that death was not the end for Jesus, nor will it be the end for us, but rather only the beginning of a potentially blissful eternity. And the season of Easter, coinciding with the coming of spring, boosts the idea that life is indeed stronger than death, that no matter how dismal the winters of our lives may be, the forces of life itself will in the end always reassert themselves.

Some may well say: 'Thank goodness we now interpret the resurrection in this way. Has Christianity in the past not been too obsessed with death and on the question of whether or not death can be overcome, whether or not we can survive it and come out triumphant on the other side? Has Christianity in the past not even tried to frighten people into believing, by harping on about the inevitability of death and the strong likelihood of punishment after death for our misdemeanours in this life? Is it not better to stress the good news of Christianity, instead of emphasising the permanently bad news of the human condition from which Christianity seeks to rescue us?' These are legitimate questions, and they may give us pause to think about the way Christianity has often been taught and preached. As a corrective to a possibly despondent and gloomy form of religion, they may well have a certain value. But they may equally well have little enough to say about the nub of the problem that today's readings present us with, which is that the 'forgiveness of sins', traditionally at the very heart of Christianity, is a notion whose meaning has, in our day, gone into a kind of exile.

It's not so much that no one believes in the reality of sin any longer, even though complaints like, 'What ever happened to sin?' or, 'Hardly anybody goes to confession any more', are often heard. It seems rather that there is doubt in at least some people's minds about God's *ability* to forgive sins. This is certainly a change from former times. You know the witticism attributed to both the Empress Catherine the Great and the German poet, Heine: 'God will forgive me. That's his job.' But nowadays, even this traditional belief is in abeyance. It's all very well to say, 'Only God can forgive sins', but that statement begs the question: 'Can even God forgive sins?' Does God have the *right* to forgive sins? What does it even mean to say that sins have been 'forgiven'?

Christianity has traditionally answered that question by pointing to the redemptive sacrifice of Christ and identifying in that 'mystery of faith' a divine act of forgiveness on a par with, indeed actually surpassing, the very act of creation. But might there not be something higher still? Might undoing the sins of the past not be something even better, even more desirable, certainly more comprehensible to our minds than the forgiveness of sins?

Christianity's answer to this agonising question – agonising, considering the litany of unbearable and unexplainable suffering and evil the past has to show for itself, a lot of it caused by human beings – is: 'No, it's not better to have the sins of the past undone than to have sins forgiven, for the simple reason that to undo or unmake the sins of the past would, presumably, amount to eradicating all of creation, to "unspeaking", as it were, the Word of Creation.' The decision to create is a decision that God, no doubt, didn't take lightly, but it was the only one, we believe, he could take if he wanted us to exist. So, to wish past sins and past evil not to have happened or to be undone is like wishing that creation had never occurred. An edited version of reality, with the horrible bits removed as if they had never existed, just doesn't seem possible.

Instead, what Christianity preaches is the 'forgiveness of sins', as the 'mystery of faith', than which 'nothing greater can be thought'.

So, in considering the implications of the Christian belief in 'the forgiveness of sins' we have to accept, I think, that the choice is between believing that God has the ability to 'forgive sins', which means accepting that he has the ability to justify his risk in creating the world – or we have to accept that it would have been better had nothing ever existed. God, we believe, can forgive sins, and thus make life worth living, but even God cannot produce an edited version of reality with the evil and suffering undone and removed.

'Poetry,' Novalis said, 'heals the wounds inflicted by reason.' That may well be so. But what Christian faith teaches is that Christ is the Word of God whose sacrifice on the cross heals the wounds inflicted by 'unreason', by wickedness and evil, and thus enables us to breathe freely again in this world. This, presumably, is at least part of what is meant by that much abused word 'spirituality'. The breath or spirit of God in us enables us to breathe freely and to live in this world by assuring us, in the words of Julian of Norwich, that 'Sin is behovely, but all shall be well and all shall be well and all manner of thing shall be well'.

RESURRECTION AND FORGIVENESS[29]

When John Henry Newman was asked why he thought Christianity was unique as a religion, he said it was because it offered the forgiveness of sins. Today's second reading is indeed specifically focused on this reality. In that second reading, St John is at pains to clarify what he means by saying that 'God is love'. He writes: 'This is the love I mean: not our love for God, but God's love for us when he sent his Son to be the sacrifice that takes our sins away.'

We might ask ourselves why the church places such a reading before us in the Easter season. Why don't we have readings today that are exclusively about the resurrection, which is what most of us would associate with the Easter season? Why doesn't the church, in other words, stress specifically today that Jesus has risen from the dead and that he has shown in this way that we too have the possibility of rising from the dead one day? That is of course part of the Christian message to the world. But there's a lot more to Christianity than the resurrection, extraordinary and important though that is, and it is to this even deeper dimension of our faith that the church wants to point us, I think, by today's readings.

The readings today, in other words, direct our attention to even weightier matters than the resurrection from the dead as such. They remind us of the reason why Jesus lived and died and rose again, which was so that sins could be forgiven and the redemption of the world could be made possible. And when the church in today's readings reminds us of Jesus' commandment to his followers to 'love one another', we are reminded that it is possible for us to try to live our lives in the light of what God has done for us in Christ, in the light of the fact that our sins have been forgiven.

But we often tend to be fixated on death and on the question of whether or not death can be negotiated, whether or not we can survive it and come out in one piece on the other side. Today's gospel reminds us that there are other important questions to be thought about, above all the question of why we would want to survive death and rise from the grave in the first place; and that can only be if we have a reason for wanting to preserve and prolong the life we have been given on this earth.

Christianity tells us that in the long run life is unbearable, indeed is not worth having, if it is marked by evil and the fruits of evil, which produce human suffering. All that has to be removed so that we can enjoy life as God intended it to be, free from sin. But our faith also tells us that we are unable to remove sin and evil and its consequences from the world. Only God himself, in the divine sacrifice of his Son, can bring about the forgiveness of sin and in that way open up the road to heaven for all of us, a road that begins here on earth and is traced out by a new way of living, a new way of being human. That at least is the ideal, but often the old ways persist and blot out the new way of Christ. The old ways, however, can never quite erase the new way inaugurated by Jesus Christ. Otherwise we wouldn't be here today to commemorate in the mass the life, death and resurrection of Jesus Christ. So, even if the way of Jesus, rather than being a description of how things actually are, serves only as a reminder to us of what could be, of what should be, it can still be said to be alive and active among us.

When we look back, then, into history and look out still at the immensity of human suffering in the world, a lot of it caused by our own inhumanity (which is another name for sin), we can begin to realise that life permanently distorted in this way is not what we are looking for in eternity, but rather what we are looking for is life cured of all suffering and evil and united to God. It's so easy, however, to take for granted that this goal is possible, and to forget that the forgiveness of sins, which makes it possible, is the heart of Christianity, and an even more incredible mystery than the very existence of the world. St John of the Cross said that it caused God more trouble redeeming the world than creating it, because he was able to create out of nothing, but to redeem it he had to sacrifice his own Son. In other words, the forgiveness of one sin is a greater deed, from God's point of view, than the creation of the world.

The great saints remind us of the simple but profound realities of our faith. It's the incomprehensible truth of redemption that we are *really* celebrating and reminding ourselves about once again in this Easter Season when we profess not just that Jesus is risen from the dead, but the reason why he came and died and rose from the dead: so we could share, freed from sin, in the reality of the life of God, who is love.

CAN THE 'BAD THIEF' BE SAVED?[30]

The gospel reading for the feast of Christ the King shows Jesus not in any regal splendour, but dying on a cross, mocked and scorned by those around him except the 'good thief'. The crucifixion scene is no doubt so powerful an image because it seems to symbolise the way the world really is, rather than the way we would like it to be. It reminds us of the countless scenes of injustice and cruelty that are played out the world over, day in and day out. And in today's world, as in the past, we hear repeatedly being addressed to God the same scornful, but often despairing questions that were addressed to Jesus on Calvary in his agony on the cross: 'Why does God not end the terrible suffering in the world? Why does he not intervene once and for all and bring justice and peace to the world?'

I don't think there are any satisfactory answers to these age-old questions. But we can perhaps learn something about how to cope with them if we look at the two criminals, or 'thieves' as they have traditionally been known, who were crucified together with Jesus. Maybe that's the best we can hope for as human beings, to find a way of living with these questions rather than despairingly seeking some neat answer to them.

The first thief is frequently written off as the 'bad thief' because of the insolent way he spoke to Jesus. It is tempting to take it for granted that we have nothing to learn from him. At most we might think he is an example of how *not* to react to the problem of injustice and suffering and death. But on reflection, was his request to Jesus really so bad? Here was a man who apparently had done a great deal of evil in his life, but who nevertheless still wanted to stay alive, despite the dire predicament he was in. The 'bad thief' saw in Jesus his last, if almost impossible chance of surviving. He does not really seem to have believed Jesus *could* save him, but he made the request anyway. The desire for life, even in harrowing circumstances, even if concealed beneath his jibe at Jesus, can hardly be such a bad thing. And is there not part of us all that is the 'bad thief'?

However, in the light of our Christian faith, the 'good thief' had a sharper and deeper insight into the reality of things, even in his desperate situation, because it was a truer insight. We might say he had come to accept that issues of justice are real, and cannot in the long run be denied or suppressed, and that justice will finally always be vindicated, even if not in this life. But as well as believing in the ultimate reality of justice, the 'good thief' must also have believed in the indisputable value of human beings, who can still be regarded as redeemable despite the evil they may do or may have done in this life. The 'good thief' had retained or had reached this belief. He believed that it was worthwhile, even in the face of his own imminent death, to think in terms of his eternal salvation, and to hope that this would still be possible for him. It is in this frame of mind he turns to Jesus and asks for redemption.

When the 'good thief' is promised the gift of paradise, just when all seemed lost for him, many will perhaps think that Jesus is just offering him a few well-meaning words of consolation to help him through his last agony. But to think this is, in fact, to believe that death is stronger than life, that evil is stronger than good, that injustice is stronger than justice, and that this created world is in fact stronger than God the creator and redeemer. Faith in Christ sees life, and death, and suffering, in another dimension. In some ways, throughout our lives, we can all relive the experience of children who wake in the middle of the night and, frightened of the dark, cry out for their father or mother. Christ is our father, Christ is our mother, who tells us that 'all shall be well, and all manner of thing shall be well'. That things shall be well for us all, the good thief in us, and the bad. This is not some empty consolation. These are words of love, and because of this love, we believe.

So, when Jesus says, 'Amen, I say to you: today you will be with me in paradise', it is as if he were saying, 'Do not be afraid. Everything is going to be all right'. And that, in turn, is a kind of echo of the words spoken by God at the beginning of creation: 'God saw all he had made, and indeed it was very good.'

Fundamentally, therefore, the story of the 'good thief' and the 'bad thief' is an occasion for acknowledging our faith in the goodness of God and his creation, and the Solemnity of Christ the King a good moment to celebrate God's ability to redeem the world from sin and death. Jesus incarnated this faith and made it real for us by his life, death and resurrection. In mass this morning, we can once again give thanks to God for the gift of life, for the gift of faith, and for this goodness that we have received from his Son, Jesus Christ, our Lord and King.

THE DOCTRINE
OF CHRIST

THE DEATH OF CHRIST AND THE 'WARPED WOOD' OF HUMANITY[1]

Today's second reading – from St Paul's first Letter to the Corinthians – gives one of the earliest accounts of the Last Supper, the event that is the foundation stone of the mass, which we are celebrating once again today on the feast of Corpus Christi, literally the feast of the body of Christ.

Sometimes people say that Christianity is a very violent and almost bloodthirsty religion because it puts such emphasis on the death, the terrible death by crucifixion of our Lord, Jesus Christ. This is an accusation, it seems to me, that we have to take seriously. But if we do take it seriously, and examine it closely, we'll see that it can be met.

Christianity is a very realistic religion: that's probably what people at least partly mean when they say it is a historical religion. It's historical or realistic because it takes historical experience seriously.

And that experience tells us that life is basically good, but it has its negative side, or as it has been said, human life is 'cut from warped wood';[2] in other words, we are all born with original sin. This reveals itself in the way, for example, no matter how well things ever seem to be going, life has an almost unerring habit of going awry. Or, as it was once put, when Adam and Eve bit into the apple in the Garden of Eden, they discovered it was sour. Perfect happiness doesn't seem to be attainable on this earth, try though we might to reach it or achieve it. Someone once expressed it in this way, using interestingly enough a violent image too: life is booby-trapped, and it's only a matter of time before you step on the one meant for you.

Be that as it may, Jesus in his own time certainly seemed to many of his followers the incarnation of the perfect life: he gave those who followed him the sense that life was good, and worth living, so much so that many even believed perfection had arrived, or was about to arrive, in the shape of the Kingdom of God. But, as we know, Jesus' earthly life did not lead to the arrival of paradise in this world but came to an abrupt and cruel end on the cross after what St Paul in today's second reading referred to as the 'night that he was betrayed'. And that dark, discordant note of betrayal has sounded throughout all of human history, when one good person or one good cause after another seems to get defeated by what St Paul on another occasion called the 'mystery of iniquity', or the mystery of evil. Jesus, too, who had given hope to so many in his own day, was betrayed and then executed in the most terrible way.

So, to take up the accusation I mentioned earlier, that Christianity is bloodthirsty, we'd have to say rather that Christianity grew out of Christ's suffering the evil of the world, as its divine victim. Far from recommending bloodletting and suffering, the Christian faith actually developed out of Christ's willingness and ability to absorb the suffering of the world, without endorsing or welcoming it and, just as significantly, without condemning the world as such for his fate. In other words, Christ showed that there was more to life and ultimate reality than an acknowledgement of the fact that suffering and evil are seemingly irremovable aspects of our world.

The secret of Christianity, in other words, is that Jesus didn't take out of an awareness of the power of evil any message of ultimate defeat or despair. On the contrary, he brought to it, or he countered it with, a message of hope and of immortality. For Jesus believed, and his followers ever since have lived out of this belief, that the reality of God, the reality of goodness, is stronger than the forces of evil, and can always eventually defeat, outwit and overcome them. A limping truth, as has been said, will always eventually overtake the fastest and most powerful lie. In going to his painful death, Jesus may have abandoned – indeed, he did abandon – his life, but not his faith in God, which was so strong that his followers came to realise that it was the same as God, that Jesus himself was divine.

So at mass we don't just recall the terrible death of Christ, but as St Paul puts it: we do so 'until the Lord comes'. That's to say, we don't just look back in every mass to the first mass at the Last Supper, which anticipated the crucifixion of Jesus, but we look back with an eye to the future, when Christ will come again, and when the resurrection will be a reality not only for Christ, but for all those who try to be guided by his way, his truth, and his life.

The feast of Corpus Christ is a feast, therefore, that has traditionally been associated not with deep sadness or mourning but with great joy and beauty, as the Corpus Christi processions throughout the world testify. The feast of Corpus Christi is a chance for us to focus again on the great and profound truths of our faith and to allow them, with God's help, to sink more and more deeply into the reality of our own lives here and now.

THE DIVINITY OF CHRIST AND THE ASSUMPTION OF MARY[3]

Today, on the feast of the Assumption of Mary into Heaven, it might perhaps be useful to think a little on what this feast means for the church. I say 'for the church', and not simply 'for us', because the reality of the mysteries of our faith is fundamentally a gift that comes to us from God through the church. The mysteries of our faith are not, in the first instance at any rate, conclusions that we could draw from reflection on our own religious experience, important though such reflection undoubtedly is, but rather have, we believe, a different origin. And that origin is in God.

Nowadays and in the history of the church it is, and has often been, maintained that Mary is a model for us. Just as Mary, the handmaid of the Lord, always obeyed God and served him faithfully, so we also should try to develop the same religious virtues in our own lives. Or sometimes we hear it said that Mary's destiny is a kind of foretaste of our own personal destiny. Just as Mary was taken up into heaven after her death, so one day we too will be able to enter heaven, and indeed not just with our soul but with both body and soul. In *that* sense, the doctrine of the Assumption of Mary, it is maintained, is a pointer to or reminder of the importance of human work or physical suffering in our earthly lives. Now, all that is perfectly correct and valid. But one might wonder whether it really gets to the heart of the matter.

The church's teaching on Mary the Mother of God, in all its aspects, has only ever really had one simple goal in mind, and that was to defend and to proclaim the humanity and the divinity of Christ. Thus, if we call Mary the Mother of God, that means that her son, Jesus, had a mother like the rest of us, and hence was truly human. But at the same time, Jesus is, Christian faith teaches, true God. The mystery of the incarnation of the Son of God happened through Mary, and is forever connected with Mary, the Mother of God. This mystery is hidden in, and protected by, and defended, because realised, by Mary.

But how, we might well ask, is this truth of our faith bound up with the Assumption of Mary? We could perhaps see a partial answer to this obvious question in the fact that the Assumption of Mary into heaven is certainly something wonderful that intimately binds Mary to Jesus, her son, who ascended into heaven after his resurrection, but it is not something that makes Mary intrinsically divine as Jesus is, as our faith professes. That must mean then that the mystery of Christ's divine sonship is something that cannot adequately be explained or understood even in terms of such extraordinary and awesome realities as the resurrection or the ascension.

The Assumption of Mary into heaven teaches us that what God has done for us in Christ is something so unimaginably great that human existence, which we believe is called to union with God, cannot be regarded as completed or perfected even by our participation in such transcendent realities as the resurrection from the dead and the assumption into heaven. That, in turn, is implied by the belief that our destiny, our final end, doesn't lie simply in the fulfilment of our own wishes and dreams – concerning, for instance, our own hopes of resurrection – but in God himself. For what would eternal life and the resurrection from the dead be, without God? It might only be undying boredom and eternal torment, as indeed the doctrine of the possibility of hell intimates.

Thus, the most important thing for us to remember, when we think about Mary and her feastdays, is not what Mary can teach us about the meaning of human existence – for instance, that we are meant to survive death – but rather what Mary, through the grace of God, has given us. It is not primarily an interesting explanation of the world or a sublime teaching about the final end of the human race that we are indebted to Mary for, but rather something much more profound and wonderful, namely the redemption of the world, accomplished for us by Mary's son, Jesus Christ, who became man that we might become God.

The Absence of Jesus and the Presence of Curiosity[4]

The story of the journey to Emmaus is a good advertisement for the advantages of talking to strangers. If the two disciples, making their way to Emmaus, had resented – as well they might have – the rather peremptory way in which a perfect stranger introduced himself into their conversation, they would have been acting in a very normal manner. But that very normality would have kept them confined to their well-tried, secure and familiar modes of understanding and behaviour that, by their own admission, had only succeeded in making them downcast and disappointed.

One of the engaging aspects of Christianity is that it is, or can be, in the best possible sense, curious: curious about itself, about its own meaning, and about others, about other religions and other people. I don't see how you can understand the many theological upheavals and disputes or the great missionary movements of the Christian church throughout its 2,000-year-old history, if you don't allow for a large dose of curiosity about the meaning of Christian faith, and an equally large dose of curiosity about what makes other people tick. That other factors and higher powers are at work as well is no doubt true, but the simple virtue of curiosity about the truth of all human existence is, I think, a vital element of Christian faith, and probably related to a deep-rooted sense of our common humanity.

So when the two disciples in today's gospel story were buttonholed by an inquisitive stranger, their reaction was not to take offence, but to welcome with some curiosity his intervention in their discussion. They didn't even take offence when he corrected their theology, a reaction that by Christian standards is almost miraculous.

But by reacting as they did, they illustrated dramatically the truth of one of the promises Jesus made to his followers: that where two or three were gathered together in his name, he would be there with them. For the two disciples were still gathered in Jesus' name as they made their way to Emmaus and discussed what had become of their former faith in Jesus and of their hopes for what he might achieve, hopes that now no longer seemed realisable.

And it is also important to see that they weren't entirely astray. When the stranger corrected them, he only said they hadn't yet accepted the *full* message of the prophets. Yet they had got a lot of things right. They had, after all, identified Jesus of Nazareth as a great prophet from God, and they had become his disciples. But what is perhaps even more significant is that in admitting the stranger into their company and conversation, they were admitting their own incomplete grasp on truth. Hence their curiosity. Only those who think they know everything cease to be curious and risk becoming ideologues.

What might save us from such a fate, as it saved the two disciples on the road to Emmaus, is to take to heart the lesson they were taught: that Jesus reached his glory through suffering. And that glory is his overcoming of the sins of the world, so that he can offer us all a share in the life of God for ever. This is the mystery of faith which we can only receive as an unexpected gift, created in a unique and unexpected way by the cross and resurrection of Jesus.

The suffering and death of Jesus may undoubtedly be a powerfully illuminating symbol of the human condition as well, but if that is all it is, then it would only be, at best, a profound piece of wisdom for us to absorb. Over and above that, we believe it is the price God paid in Christ for our redemption. As such it must remain a mystery, as the resurrection primordially is and will always remain a mystery. And in the deepest sense Jesus too must always remain a stranger, who, when recognised by faith, disappears, as at Emmaus, and never becomes our possession. Similarly, to be able to recognise Christ in the eucharist means accepting his absence there in historical form.

But the recognition of who Jesus really is, is for us, as for the two Emmaus disciples, the saving grace of the Christian reality which, when genuine, will generate warmth and light in the world. The Emmaus story, whatever else it communicates, strongly suggests that if religious faith makes us downcast, gloomy and disappointed, then that faith is certainly not useless or phoney, but it is still in need of being transformed. The fact that the church has given the Emmaus story a permanent place in the three-year liturgical cycle springs, one may suppose, from a realisation that its message always needs to be relearned, just as our faith, like that of the first believers, always needs to be transformed. Let's hope that when the opportunities for such transformation occur, we'll be able to see and to seize them.

THE KINGDOM
OF HEAVEN

THE VIOLENCE OF LIFE AND THE KINGDOM OF HEAVEN[1]

The strange saying contained in the gospel we've just heard, 'that from the time of John the Baptist until now the kingdom of heaven has been subjected to violence and the violent take it by force', is not easy to interpret. Maybe even impossible. Its original meaning may now be lost, though not its evocative potential, as is shown by the use Flannery O'Connor made of it in the title of one of her most powerful works, *The Violent Bear It Away*.

The phrase could be understood perhaps as an invitation of sorts to us not to take any form of human misfortune or injury too seriously, seeing that violence can even be done to the kingdom of heaven itself.[2] The New Testament indeed claims that even God suffered violence and ultimately death when he attempted to live in this world. But the New Testament also claims that God's kingdom is indestructible in the long term, even if it's not immune from violence in the short term. And this in turn suggests that it is worthwhile waiting patiently for God to come to us, as we do pre-eminently in the season of Advent.

Someone who knew the value of waiting patiently for God was the saint whose feastday we celebrate today: St John of the Cross. He suffered violence not, as it happens, from the world, but from his own religious order when he set out to reform it. But some of his greatest poetry, it seems, was written in his time of greatest suffering, because he was always sustained by a faith in God that guided him more surely than the light of this world, whether the light of the senses or even of the mind.

In what's left of Advent, indeed in what's left of our time on earth, we're invited to concentrate on the reality and closeness of God and to look forward, beyond the violence of this world, to the triumph of God's goodness and mercy and glory.

THE DARK SIDE OF THE BEATITUDES[3]

Today's gospel contains Jesus' frequently quoted sermon on the beatitudes that is often taken as the very heart of Christian moral teaching. We often, naturally enough, pay attention to the positive side of this sermon, and remember especially the consoling words Jesus speaks to those who are life's underdogs, those who always get the rough end of the stick, who never seem to reach a position where they can enjoy life, who are always hassled by the difficulties and worries of life. To such people Jesus promises consolation, relief from hardship and the enjoyment of the kingdom of heaven.

But there is also a darker side to Jesus' message. He has harsh words to say about those whose behaviour frequently makes life so painful for others. There could scarcely be a more damning contrast than that between those who, in Jesus' view, seem to be life's winners and those who seem to be life's losers. Jesus is saying that one day there will be a dramatic reversal of this situation. The underdogs are finally going to triumph, and those who ruled the roost for their own benefit are finally going to come a cropper.

Yet Jesus' words do raise an important and thorny question. And it might be put like this: in making such a strident contrast between two groups of people, is Jesus perhaps encouraging the very things he seeks to condemn? In condemning the rich, those who know nothing of hunger, those whose lives are full of laughter, not sorrow, is he not perhaps, even if unwittingly, encouraging those whom life has treated badly to look with hatred and resentment on those whose lives seem to be going so well? And is this not the very opposite of what we normally think of as the essence of Christian morality, namely that we should love even our enemies and those who do us harm?

There is, I think, no easy answer to this kind of question, and here again we find in the gospels the very ambiguity of life itself, the very lack of any clear solution to life's moral dilemmas. And that's maybe one of the reasons why the gospels have fascinated people down through the centuries, because while they do proclaim and announce redemption through Christ, they don't offer any easy answers to the messiness of human existence. Perhaps in a passage like the one we've just heard in the gospel today, Jesus wants us to realise and to feel in our own bones just how closely good and evil actually are to each other. He maybe wants us to understand that in becoming indignant, and rightly so, at evil and suffering in the world, we can become hate-filled ourselves against those perpetrating evil and injustice. It's all very well to talk about hating the sin but loving the sinner, but in practice it's hard to maintain that division. And then when we go a step beyond indignation and try to remove evil and hatred and injustice, do we not run the risk of falling into these very same sins ourselves?

And yet Jesus' words can't be played down, or brushed aside or swept under the carpet. God is good and just, and he can't simply turn a blind eye to the evil and suffering of the world. There has to be some compensation for those who have suffered in life. What Christianity teaches us, however, is that the compensation comes not from us in the form of vengeance, but from God himself, who in Jesus Christ, the lamb of God, took the sins of the world upon himself and made up for all the evil ever done or ever to be done. The resurrection of Jesus, at the centre of the second reading, is the sign that God has the capacity to overcome evil and injustice in his own way, the way of self-sacrifice, and to rise triumphant from the dead. And, in the final analysis, in so far as we can ever reach a final analysis in this life or indeed in any other, this is what our Christian faith encourages us to believe: not that we should be or are morally better than others – often we're not – but to believe that Jesus has overcome evil and suffering, and risen victorious from the dead and thus made life, eternal life even, the life of the kingdom of heaven possible for all of us.

THE KINGDOM OF HEAVEN IS NO LAUGHING MATTER[4]

A former Anglican archbishop of Dublin in the nineteenth century, Richard Whately, once wrote that 'Happiness is no laughing matter'. After listening to the parable in today's gospel about a king who wanted to give a feast for his son's wedding, you can see why the archbishop might have written what he did. The parable of the royal wedding feast is, we are told, a symbol of the kingdom of heaven. Indeed Jesus himself is portrayed as saying as much in today's gospel. We are also told that the first group of invited guests who turned down their invitations, and the second group, who, in some cases, went a big step further and murdered those reminding them of their invitations, refer to the Jewish people who refused to accept Christ, and as a punishment were to have their city, Jerusalem, destroyed by the Romans in AD 70. Those who eventually turn up for the wedding feast are then said to symbolise the gentiles who came into the church after the refusal of so many Jews to do so. And, finally, the detail of the guest who had no wedding garment is supposed to teach us that being in the kingdom of heaven, even for gentiles, brings its own obligations: in other words, unless we can show good works, represented by the wearing of a wedding garment, we will not be allowed to participate. In short, even in the kingdom of heaven there's no such thing as a free lunch.

Now, it may well be true that the parable of the royal wedding feast in today's gospel reflects tensions between the early Christians and their Jewish neighbours, and maybe even reflects frustration and exasperation on the part of the infant church at the seeming unwillingness of so many to see the light presented by Christianity. But that still leaves us, nearly 2,000 years on, with the question of how to understand and make sense of this parable today.

And the problem of understanding it is much wider, I think, than simply trying to work out the proper relationship between Christians and Jews, vitally important though that huge question is. But the wider and deeper question this parable surely raises for us is to try to understand why, if the kingdom of heaven is such a wonderful thing, as Isaiah says in today's first reading, does it seem to be so unattractive? Why do so many people seem so uninterested in it? Why do they almost have to be pestered into taking note of it? Why, indeed, do they often react violently and even murderously against invitations to be involved with it? Why does the divine offer of a share in God's life lead not to unalloyed joy and happiness but, in the parable of the royal wedding feast, to violence, war and suffering? Today's gospel may begin by speaking about the kingdom of heaven, but it goes on to talk about murder and destruction, and ends up talking about 'the dark, where there will be weeping and grinding of teeth' – an expression, incidentally, that Matthew seems quite attached to: he uses it six times in his gospel.

Now, it could well be that Matthew likes employing shock tactics to get his message across. But still, it is a bit strange to attempt to convince people that it is desirable to be in the kingdom of heaven by threatening them with dire consequences if they don't take up the offer. It's almost like saying: 'If you don't allow me to make you happy, I'm going to kill you.' And unfortunately, the use of force, even of lethal force in the spreading of the Christian message, has not been unknown in church history, even though we may not exactly wish to blame the New Testament for encouraging such lapses. However, the least we would seem forced to admit is that religion is a dangerous business; and maybe that's only because life itself is a dangerous business, so dangerous in fact that even God cannot remove the risks involved in his creation, whether those risks are tied to the potential for natural catastrophes that seems endemic to this world, or whether they come from the way we ourselves can abuse the freedom we have been born with.

But yet, despite knowing all this, God thought it worthwhile to go ahead and create us, and despite all the horrors of human history, God can, in his Son Jesus Christ, still speak of the kingdom of heaven as the glorious end for which everything was created. Maybe that's more important for us to focus on than the failures we may have so far chalked up in trying to embody that kingdom in our own lives. After 2,000 years, the message is still the same, the offer still stands, the kingdom of heaven, enacted by the sacrifice of Christ, is still a reality. Our difficulties in understanding what the kingdom of heaven really is are surely less important and less serious than God's determination to make it a reality for us. Or, to put it another way, what we think or don't think about God is ultimately of much less significance than what God thinks about us, and of infinitely less significance than what God has done for us in Christ and promised to give us in fullness at the end of time.

TIME AND ETERNITY[5]

A lesson we can all learn from today's gospel reading about the Transfiguration of the Lord is that the blinding truths of life usually only come to us, if at all, on rare occasions. Most of the time, grey, monotonous, repetitive reality is the order of the day. Thus, the three apostles in today's gospel were able to see the Transfiguration of Jesus for a very short time, but then straight away everyday reality took over again, and the revelation of a profound truth was withdrawn from them. This raised for them and raises still for us the question: what is the connection between an experience like the Transfiguration and everyday existence? Or in simpler language: what is the connection between time and eternity?

Eternity, presumably, cannot just mean an infinite amount of time, an endless series of minutes, hours, days, weeks, months and years – marked only by 'the eternal return of the same'. In a short story by the Argentinian writer, Jorge Luis Borges, entitled 'The Immortal', an image is conjured up of a race of people who enjoyed immortality, but, having had time to do everything that could possibly be done, they had lapsed into a permanent state of lethargy, unable to muster any enthusiasm for any specific activity. For them, the gift of immortality had simply turned out to be the gateway to infinite apathy. In Christian understanding, however, hope for 'the life of the world to come' (*et exspecto … vitam venturi saeculi*, as the Creed puts it), has never been confined to the hope of overcoming death. Eternal life or immortality, in other words, doesn't simply mean, as far as Christianity is concerned, an endless continuation or prolongation of earthly existence, because this existence first has to be transfigured or redeemed in order to be heavenly or divine, in order for it to be able to participate fully in the life of God.

At the same time, however, we probably wouldn't have any interest at all in eternal life if we hadn't already found or experienced in this life something that we would like to take with us into eternity or that we would dearly love to find there. The question, then, is, 'what is there on this earth that we would like to enjoy for all eternity?' Most people would probably say that the answer to that question has to be 'Love'. Christians can say further that God is Love itself. Whoever experiences love in any genuine sense has experienced something of the reality of God. We can go on to say that divine love has become visible and palpable, has indeed become human for us in Jesus Christ. But what is the relationship between this divine reality of love and the suffering and sadness and 'untransfigured' nature of so much of human history? In view of the misery of so much human history, which today's gospel also alludes to by pointing to the death of Jesus, which was the end in store for him in Jerusalem, how can we speak of the God who made this world as love?

Our faith teaches us that we are unfortunately, or maybe fortunately,[6] not able to explain everything. Our faith, however, also points to Jesus, who is God and man, who has not explained the suffering and sin of the world. But he is the Lamb of God who by his death and resurrection has taken away the sin of the world, and in doing so has given our history, and given us, the possibility of being transfigured one day in the kingdom of heaven, just as Jesus himself was raised from the indignity of his own death and taken to sit at the right hand of the Father in glory. Out of this inexplicable mystery of our faith we can continue to draw hope for our future and forgiveness for our past. Our perseverance in faith already is a little piece of heaven on earth; it's a small but genuine reflection of eternity in time. Our permanent refusal to acknowledge or acquiesce in or accept the rightness of evil and suffering is a kind of 'negative image of eternity' (Gerd Theissen) that can guide us like a faithful star towards heaven.

In and with and through Jesus Christ a few people of his time discovered something that they didn't ever want to lose again, something that they wanted to last for ever. These followers of Jesus handed on their faith to those who came after them, and by a long and often painful process it has come down to us. This mystery is the mystery of our faith in Jesus Christ, the only mystery that can continue to light up human hearts and bring eternal light and eternal warmth and eternal hope into our often dismal world. We now have the opportunity in our own time to carry forward and hand on this mystery of our faith to those around us and to those who will come after us.

THE RELIEF OF NOT BEING RESPONSIBLE[7]

Today, the third Sunday of Advent, is traditionally known as *Gaudete* Sunday, or the 'Sunday for rejoicing'. It's the Sunday when the church's liturgy highlights the mood of hope and expectation that Advent evokes, in anticipation of Christmas. For where there's hope, there's at least the makings of joy. But where there's no hope, there's no joy; there is, at most, only regret, regret for a past that is closed and cannot be re-opened. Hope, on the other hand, is directed to a future that is still open. And also still open, of course, is the question of whether what lies ahead of us, beyond death, is better than what we now have.

So, all things considered, on this *Gaudete* Sunday, should we be jumping for joy at the thought of our future prospects, or succumbing to the sadness of regret for a bungled or maybe just an indifferent, but now vanished past? Before we answer that question, we might recall, as someone once remarked, that if you do jump for joy, you should make sure nobody moves the ground from beneath your feet.[8] And there's the rub. Joy may exact a high price. On the one hand, today's gospel reading leaves us in no doubt about the prize to be won in the kingdom of heaven. It is so unimaginably great that to get in anywhere, to be even the least in that kingdom, is still to be greater than John the Baptist, who himself was, in Christ's own words, the greatest 'of all the children born of women'. Who wouldn't jump at such a prize? Who wouldn't love to get it? But, on the other hand, if we do embrace the Christian faith wholeheartedly, then it demands in principle everything from us, the sacrifice of all we have and all we are, for the sake of the kingdom of heaven. It demands, if necessary, the ultimate sacrifice of life itself, which the martyrs all made. But is such a demand too high? Is such a sacrifice too great? Why should ordinary mortals be asked to show such love?

Questions of that nature have made many people wonder about Christianity before today. They've wondered whether the Christian faith is just too sublime, too idealistic, too far beyond most normal people to be a realistic option, except perhaps as a now acceptable, because inevitable, form of hypocrisy or compromise. And such people may have a point. But the strange paradox of Christianity is that, despite all the talk about the demands that it makes and that have in fact been accepted and fulfilled in the past by many of the faithful, it doesn't really seem to matter what we do for God in the long run. It's what God does for us that counts. That's to say, if being the least in the kingdom of heaven is better than even living and dying like John the Baptist, who sacrificed his freedom and his life for God, then whatever the kingdom of heaven is, it's not something that even the highest human sacrifice can ever bring into being.

Where, you might well ask, does that leave John the Baptist? Was he sold a dummy? Was he taken for a ride? Well, of course not. But if we believe he now is in the kingdom of heaven, then it must be not because of what he himself did and suffered, but because of what God in Christ has done for all humanity in taking away the sins of the world by his death on the cross and opening up permanently for us the gates of heaven. The gates of heaven are now open permanently because just as no human excellence, not even John the Baptist's, could have opened up heaven for us, so no human depravity, we believe, can ever close it again.

The Christian church is the body that carries this saving truth through history. But the church only carries this truth – it's not identical with it, any more than a mother is identical with the child she carries in her womb. In that sense the title 'Holy Mother Church', which can sometimes sound a bit quaint in today's world, points us to a profound truth that is both heartening and chastening. For the reality of Christ *is* kept alive in the church, but since it is also true that the divine saviour in the womb of Holy Mother Church cannot survive outside it, there will always be a painful disparity between the church which we flawed human beings present to the world, and the divine treasure within, which we have the privilege of protecting and handing on.

But, maybe even that isn't such bad news, if it relieves us – as it should – of the responsibility for salvation. Salvation, the church teaches us, is from Christ, not from us, and it's that life-giving teaching which allows us to rejoice in this season of Advent. For in rejoicing we are not blowing our own trumpet or crowing over our own achievements, but giving thanks to God who, for reasons best known to himself, has called us out of nothingness into existence and who came to join us as a child 2,000 years ago in Bethlehem in order to bring us to heaven.

It may be an instinctive sense of the incongruity of the Incarnation, which seems almost to echo the incongruity of creation itself, that has made Christmas into the quintessentially Christian celebration in our world, whatever theological purists may say. If that is true, then it shows that God's unfathomable and surprising life-giving goodness, which encourages our hope, can still make Christianity a compelling and inextinguishable light for the world.

BETWEEN HEAVEN AND EARTH

THE MIRACLE OF TRANSFORMATION[1]

The story of the wedding feast at Cana is one of the best-known episodes in the gospels, probably because of the appeal all stories that deal with the mystery of change or transformation have for us. This story seems to encapsulate a general truth, or a general hope anyway, about human existence, because people generally believe that they have appeared on earth not just to exist and die, but for some deeper purpose. In this sense, the transformation of water into wine by Jesus at the wedding feast of Cana speaks to the deep and seemingly inextinguishable belief human beings have that, by his grace, God has the ability and the desire to transform the water of our ordinary, often humdrum or painful lives, into the wine of his own heavenly existence. Or in other words, that we have been created, as the old catechism put it, to know, love and serve God here on earth, and be happy with him for ever in heaven.

The question arises, though: if God wishes to offer us the wine of heaven, why can't he do it more obviously, here and now? To use the images of the wedding feast at Cana: we can see enough water in life, but where is the wine? We can see so much suffering and unhappiness in life, but where is the wine of heavenly happiness?

The only partial answer the church has ever offered to this difficult and unsettling question is to say that heaven is certainly a gift God offers us, but we have to make some effort in order to receive it. While grace, as an ancient Christian adage has it, presupposes and builds on nature, nature has to cooperate with grace in the process of our redemption. The paradox, then, seems to be that while our natural existence, as far as we are concerned, is given to us completely gratuitously, our God-given salvation cannot apparently be achieved in us without some contribution from our side. This may strike us as a tall order. We might think, what can we do to make heaven a reality? But we can be encouraged by the transformation story of the wedding feast at Cana, for we can learn that even wine cannot exist without water; that water, humble water, is a basic commodity contained in the substance of wine. And we might note in passing that the water used at Cana was not even drinking water, but only very ordinary water used for washing rituals.

So, we can take heart from the story of the wedding feast at Cana and realise that God honours us, as it were, by letting the apparent humble ordinariness of our human lives become a fundamental ingredient in the reality of the glory of heaven, without which heaven wouldn't exist. Or to put this in perhaps more familiar language, divine grace would have no effect in our lives if humble human nature didn't exist to be transformed by grace in the first place. And our contribution towards making the glory of heaven a reality for us is to accept and live the earthly life God has given us, harsh and burdensome though it may often be. In doing so, we can be confident that, as Jesus turned the water of Cana into wine, God will also turn the water of our lives into the wine of heaven.

WHAT IS A PARISH?[2]

Every year the Forty Hours' Adoration is held at this time of year in this church [The Church of the Sacred Heart, Belfast]. The reason, of course, is that the feast of the Sacred Heart – which we celebrated two days ago on Friday – always marks year by year the start of the Forty Hours' Adoration in our parish. The feast of the Sacred Heart is also the day which reminds us all specifically of the name of our parish, and even more so it points us directly to the divine reality in whose name our parish was founded exactly one hundred years ago this year.

It's interesting, I think, to remember on an occasion like this just what the word 'parish' means. Because the term 'parish' and, even more so, the term 'parochial' have come to mean in our language something narrow or inward-looking or provincial, whereas nothing could be further from the truth. The word 'parish', which is a specifically Christian word, originally referred to those who lived alongside other people in the world, but were not themselves entirely of this world, and weren't entirely absorbed by it; they had in fact much wider horizons than those of their fellow citizens who may have lived only in and for this world. The early Christians, in their parishes, regarded themselves as little colonies of heaven on earth because they believed that, though they were born into this world, their ultimate destiny lay with God. Hence for the original Christian 'parishioners', the sky – or heaven – was the limit. Heaven was their true home, and living in 'parishes' reminded them constantly of this basic, essential ingredient of their faith. Their vision was anything but 'parochial' in the negative or narrow modern sense.

It is these simple, but profound Christian truths that I am so grateful to this parish for passing on to me. I was born into this parish and grew up in it, was baptised in this church, made my First Holy Communion here, was confirmed here, and had the privilege of being ordained a priest here almost thirty years ago to the day. It was the people of this parish – priests and laity alike – who passed on the truths of the faith to me as to countless others over the years, and without the enduring, unpretentious commitment of those who have gone before us, as the first eucharistic prayer has it, 'marked with the sign of faith', without their commitment, I and so many others would have grown up without the pearl of great price that our Catholic, Christian faith is.

The heart of that faith – the Sacred Heart of that faith – we celebrate in the eucharist, as we did these past few days in the special Forty Hours' Adoration. The eucharist is at the heart of our faith because it makes present the reality of God for us in our day-to-day lives, and that reality is the truth that God so loved the world that he sent his only Son, Jesus Christ, into the world, not to condemn us but to save us. 'The Sacred Heart of Jesus is the human heart of God' (Herbert McCabe), which can never stop loving the world and which nothing in the world can ever undermine or destroy. God's love for the world cannot even be destroyed by the greatest human disasters and horrors we can imagine – and, speaking of horrors, this parish has sadly had more than its fair share of suffering, death and destruction in the course of its one-hundred-year history. The struggle of people here to keep faith with their basic beliefs over the years was not endured without much suffering. But faith in God's love for the world, embodied in the powerful symbol of the Sacred Heart of Jesus, and faith in the ultimate triumph of God's ways over the frequent chaos of human ways, gave the people of this parish, as of many other parishes, the fortitude to endure and to survive. In that sense, nothing would seem to be further from the truth than Unamuno's provocative assertion, directed against the Jesuits' promotion of the cult of the Sacred Heart, which he presumably saw as encouraging supine passivity in the face of suffering, that 'hierocardiocracy' (literally, 'rule of the Sacred Heart') signified 'the tomb of the Christian religion'.[3]

The eucharist, however, doesn't just remind us of Christ's sacrifice, nor does it just sustain us in our daily lives as we go through this world – important though all this certainly is – but the eucharist is also a sign of what we are all going to be sometime in the future. After the consecration at mass, we proclaim: 'Christ has died, Christ is risen, Christ will come again.' Maybe we aren't always sufficiently attentive to that last part of the proclamation of faith. Christ, we believe, will come again, wherever we happen to be at that point, in order to bring us to heaven. The destiny, the incredible destiny we are all called to share in, is, in some incomprehensible sense, to be God ourselves, to share in God's own life as members of the body of Christ. The body of Christ is the eucharist. The body of Christ is also all of us who are joined to Christ in the church through the sacraments and whose final destination is heaven where we hope to see God face to face and to be happy with him for ever – and not just because we want to, but, much more importantly, because we believe that that is what God wants and has always wanted even from before the creation of the world.

So, on an evening like this, it is good to remind ourselves of these inexhaustible and liberating truths of our faith, which we could meditate on for ever without fully understanding them. But it doesn't matter if we don't fully understand them. The peace that God offers us surpasses all understanding, just as the love he showed for us in Christ surmounts and will continue to surmount all obstacles that can ever be raised against it. So, as Jesus often reminded his followers: 'There's no need to be afraid.' And, as one of the great medieval mystics, Julian of Norwich, who herself had a deep devotion to the Sacred Heart of Jesus, put it: 'All shall be well and all shall be well and all manner of thing shall be well.'

FISHING FOR GOD[4]

One thread running through the three readings of this morning's mass is the overwhelming sense of unworthiness and even worthlessness that can afflict human beings when they are confronted with the reality of the living God. Even today, in an ostensibly more secularised world than that of antiquity when Judaism and Christianity emerged, the sense of human insignificance, insecurity and apparent nothingness can deeply affect and move people who wouldn't necessarily think of themselves as believers in any 'god' or followers of any religion. For the simple truth is that the fragility and ambiguity and unpredictability of the human condition transcends the difference between believers and non-believers, and confers paradoxically a kind of stability, or at least consistency, on the fundamental features of our uncertain existence.

But the trouble with a feeling of unworthiness is that it can so easily be perverted into a kind of self-serving servility and obsequiousness before anyone or anything perceived as being more powerful than us. Hence Nietzsche's jibe that 'he who humbles himself, wants to be exalted'.[5] Now, while it would be presumptuous to judge anyone in such a deep, and personal, and sensitive area as religious piety, it is also clear that human ambition can be concealed, even in religion, 'under the sheep's clothing of humility'.[6] So rather than speak about a feeling of unworthiness before God, it might be closer to the mark, or at least more in tune with modern sensibilities, if, in thinking about the profound sense of unworthiness that Isaiah or Simon Peter or St Paul experienced in their own times, we were to use terms like fraud or charlatan. For anyone who wishes to speak to other human beings about God and doesn't have the feeling of being a complete charlatan would be best advised to say nothing. Wasn't it a Chinese sage who said it's better to be thought a fool by remaining silent than to prove yourself one by speaking?

On the other hand, Christianity has always had a soft spot for fools and even described the deepest wisdom of God as foolishness. So, while the Bible often reminds us not to speak glibly about the mysterious ways of God, it also encourages us to trust in God, and not to fear, just because God is beyond us, that he is mischievous or malevolent or playing with us as a cat might play with a mouse.

That, I think, is what the Bible in general, and today's gospel reading in particular, is urging us to accept. We are being encouraged, whatever about any initial misgivings, to believe and to act on the belief that God is not only holy, mysterious and inscrutable, but that he is good, and good to us despite the evil we do. Simon Peter, the so-called rock on which the Christian church was finally to be built, is portrayed in this morning's gospel as being himself hesitant, to put it mildly, when faced with the peremptory command from Jesus to go fishing. And he was probably quite right to be sceptical. After all, Simon Peter was an experienced fisherman, Jesus a carpenter. But the miraculous catch of fish reveals to Simon Peter that there is more to life than work, even extremely useful and successful work, or if you like, that there are bigger fish to catch than those with which he has hitherto been concerned.

Now, admittedly, 'fishing for men' – which Jesus tells Simon Peter is what he will henceforth be doing – does sound distinctly fishy in the contemporary world. But what the gospel surely means here is that the faith Jesus persuaded his followers to take on and to live with was a belief in the infinite value of human existence, a belief that, in order to be true, had to mean that human existence already shared in, and could one day even more fully share in, the infinite reality of God. This faith is, however, a good deal more demanding and frustrating than fishing, because while you can be reasonably confident that there are still some fish in the lakes and rivers and seas of our world, it's not always so easy to believe that there is a divine image in oneself or – dare I say it? – in others worth fishing for. Small wonder, if many give up in despair or disgust and go back to fishing in what they think are more profitable waters.

But Simon Peter and his companions didn't, and they managed to pass on their faith, and it has come down to us today in what is undoubtedly the longest fishing expedition in history. The reality of Jesus Christ, which they passed on to us, can still fascinate human beings like an irresistible bait. Even those who don't believe in God can be charmed by the freedom, tact, subtlety, wisdom and endurance of Jesus and the faith he inspired in his followers. If nothing else – and it's already an enormous amount – Jesus' life and above all his suffering and 'ignominious death' on the cross became 'a symbol whereby man gained a penetrating insight into his own destiny'.[7] And even the distortions of this symbol, twisting it in the fateful direction of a positive encouragement of, or connivance at, suffering as intrinsically good – which, in modern times, may have lain behind the disdain of a Goethe[8] or a Nietzsche[9] for the symbol of the cross – cannot finally undermine its undeniable, potent human truth.

You might agree with this, and yet ask: has something not been left out? What about the resurrection of Jesus? It was, after all, the resurrection of Jesus that the early Christians proclaimed, not simply his sacrifice and death for our salvation. This is, of course, perfectly true. But resurrection only makes good sense in a particular story. It was the kind of person Jesus was that made his resurrection good news and worth believing in. Resurrection is a bit like getting up in the morning, to take a very attenuated comparison. If you have nothing to get up for, waking up after a night's sleep can be a mini-disaster, whereas if you do have a reason for living, waking up can be the welcome rediscovery of the incredible fluke of our own existence, which we can continue to enjoy for a little while longer.

Resurrection can, then, only make sense for us if we want to rise from the dead. And we will only want to rise from the dead if we have found something in life that we would like to enjoy for all eternity. Christian faith believes, in the light of Jesus' destiny, that, contrary to so many appearances, human life does have a deathless quality, which not even sin can destroy. That is at least part of what we mean by saying God can forgive sin. So even death not only can be endured, but it is worth enduring for the sake of what can continue beyond it, resurrected and refreshed, we believe, by grace. For if you want or love something badly enough, you'll endure any hardship in order to get it or preserve it, even the pain of death. The divine victory over sin and death, realised in Jesus, is what we celebrate in every mass. And in doing so we recall and reaffirm with awe and wonder our connection with God who not only created us, but in Jesus gave a new and inexhaustible depth to the mystery of our humanity.

The Dullness of the Means and the Glory of the End[10]

Someone once said that he didn't mind dying, but it was the thought of being dead for so long that worried him. That puts sharply the question all religion deals with, namely: what is going to be our final end and destiny? Do we end at the grave, or do we somehow continue, and if we do continue, then in what form? Is it just more of the same, which some people might be happy enough with, or is it a transformation that awaits us, and if it is a transformation, is it a transformation for the better or for the worse?

People of Jesus' time – or some of them anyway – thought they had found a precious clue about such matters in Jesus Christ. They believed that his way of living and thinking was special and unique, and indeed unsurpassable, and after his resurrection they were convinced that his was a quality of life that continued, transformed for the better, beyond death.

If we accept this, then it is indeed hard to fathom what Jesus is up to in cases like today's gospel. For when Peter, as we might put it, makes an inspired guess or identifies Jesus correctly as the Christ of God, Jesus implicitly agrees with him, but then he orders him not to tell anyone anything about it. You might also recall how often in the gospels we are told that Jesus cured people and straight away said to them, indeed ordered them, *not* to tell anybody about it.

We might be inclined to think in relation, at least, to today's gospel, that if Jesus really is the Christ of God, and has come to show us the way to God, why does he not want people to talk about it? Why not indeed? And we in our day, are we supposed to keep quiet about our faith in Jesus Christ too? Why all this apparent secrecy? That is, I think, a good question, to which I have no satisfactory answer. However, when you consider how easy it is for religion to be misunderstood, you might be inclined to be more sympathetic to Jesus' concern for secrecy and even mystery. For the unfortunate truth is that with religion, as with every other good aspect of human existence, our enthusiasm can often get in the way of a deeper appreciation of what is really at stake. So we have to treat our religious faith with great care.

If we're too direct about religion, if Jesus had been too direct about religion, if he had allowed himself to become a kind of folk hero or pop star, he might well have won short-term adulation and success, being mobbed by the crowds everywhere he went, but what use would that have been? He might just have ignited a series of straw fires. And such straw fires might only have distracted people from the true, eternal light of God, which is the real, lasting light we want to find, which can warm and illuminate our hearts as we go through life, and which can guide us to eternal happiness at the end of time. That is the long-term interest Jesus had, and wished to pass on to his followers. And whether or not we reach the long-term goal of eternal happiness will depend more on the way we live and treat one another in this world than on any sporadic, short-lived enthusiasms we may have from time to time about God. Such enthusiasms may make us feel better for a short while, but they usually won't last too long and mightn't make much profound difference to our lives or anyone else's either. Now, you might object and say that Jesus did in fact have crowds following him around, mobbing him like a modern-day celebrity. And that is of course true. That is indeed what the gospels tell us. But they also tell us that when it came to the crunch, when the chips were down, the crowds melted away. Where were the enthusiastic crowds at Calvary? Jesus died almost completely abandoned by his followers, by even his closest followers. So it is not the fine, enthusiastic feelings, even the happy feelings that religion occasionally inspires in us that count in our Christian faith. Peter and his companions may well have felt very happy to see in Jesus the Christ of God and may have enjoyed sharing their convictions with others. And that is fine as far as it goes. But the point is that it may not go far enough. For what concerns Jesus far more in today's gospel is summed up in the following words: 'Anyone who wants to save his life will lose it; but anyone who loses his life for my sake, that man will save it.'

In other words, it is by taking up our cross and carrying it, even when – perhaps *especially* when – we don't feel any enthusiasm for the task, it is this attitude and practice which would ultimately seem to be of more importance than the passing joys religion may sometimes give us, encouraging though these joys may well be. Why the glory of heaven should be attained by the dullness of earthly fidelities is something of a paradox. It certainly wouldn't be Christianity's only paradox. Perhaps it is a sign that the glory of heaven has little enough to do with the flamboyant attractions of this world, and much to do with the ultimate value of those whom Jean-Paul Sartre described as 'hell' – other people – and how we treat them in the light of God's promise to bring them to heaven.

KEEPING ONE'S NERVE ABOUT THE FUTURE[11]

In today's second reading from the Letter to the Philippians, St Paul evokes a very important aspect of our Christian faith when he says towards the end of that reading: 'I forget the past and I strain ahead for what is still to come.' As far as Paul is concerned, the future, we'd have to say, seems to be a good deal more important than the past. And for the Christian faith, this perspective on life has in fact, over the course of the centuries, established itself as the way we should evaluate the relative importance of past and future.

But it's also true to say that in recent centuries this side of the Christian faith has often been called into question, in the sense that Christianity has often been accused of putting excessive emphasis on the future, to the neglect not only of the past but even of the present. Christianity has been accused of directing our attention only to what happens in the future, to what happens above all after death. And the insinuation, or the implicit accusation against Christianity, has been that this has been done in order to distract people's attention from the frequently unjust conditions they have to endure in this life and to fob them off with the promise of a reward in another world, while making it possible for those whose lives are very comfortable in the here and now to continue enjoying life at other people's expense.

Now it may indeed be true that faith in life after death was sometimes exploited in an unworthy fashion in order to enable or even encourage people to turn a blind eye to their neighbours' distress. Instead of being helped to improve their appalling economic and social conditions, people in need were often simply told to put up with their lot, because their reward would be great in heaven. In that way, injustice was often ignored, and misery approved of and no serious effort was made to rectify wrongs and try to change the harsh conditions many had to live in.

Yet it's important to distinguish here between a belief and the misuse or abuse or even the misunderstanding of that belief. Christianity does certainly stress the meaning and significance of life after death. But genuine Christian faith has only ever emphasised the importance of life after death or of eternal life because it believes that eternal life brings about the fulfilment of whatever it is that we find good and valuable in *this* life. Eternal life in itself would be of no interest to us if it had nothing to do with this life, or if it didn't or couldn't make eternal whatever it is that we find good and valuable in this life.

Jesus allowed the woman he met in today's gospel story, the woman caught in adultery, to appreciate the value of her life by allowing her to sense the importance and the possibilities of her own future, despite the reality of her past. For if the life of this woman had been worthless and valueless, then Jesus wouldn't have bothered referring to her future at all, which he does implicitly when he tells her to 'go away and sin no more'.

In the forty days of Lent we all have the opportunity of reflecting again on our own past and future and trying to assess the true meaning of both, in the light of the mercy of God, who in his Word Jesus Christ became human with us so that we could become divine with him. If we use this opportunity, then we can perhaps more easily resist the temptation to remain imprisoned in the past or, worse still, to keep others imprisoned in the past as a kind of sterile punishment for past errors or sins, like the strict, hypocritical accusers of the woman in today's gospel, those hypocritical accusers who seemingly wanted only to punish the woman caught in adultery and thus make her an easy scapegoat for their own sins or perhaps frustrations or disappointments in life.

If we can forget the past, if we can forget, in St Paul's sense, what lies behind us, then we can move towards our future with more hope, because in our future, which is still open, and not in our past, which is already closed, we can seek out and, as our faith assures us, we can also find the truth and fulfilment of our lives that God in his goodness wills for us.

THE GREAT TEMPTATION[12]

The advice that Jesus gives us in today's gospel with great insistence and great persuasive power is undoubtedly good, indeed irreproachable advice. And it is also certain that our world would look very different if we were all to live in accordance with the counsels of perfection that Jesus urges on us today. For in that case, God's will would not only be done in heaven, but it would also be done on earth, and we would be living in a kind of paradise.

But we know that the world in fact does not look like paradise. We pray certainly in the Our Father that God's will be done on earth as it is in heaven, but so far at least this has not come about. From time to time, some individual people do, of course, carry out the will of God in particular circumstances, but even they can't do God's will all the time. As scripture has it, even the just man falls seven times a day.

So, we can see clearly that there is always a gap, if not a gulf, between what we would like to be, and what we in fact are, between the way we'd like the world to be and the way it actually is. And for this reason, the question or the suspicion often arises in many people's minds whether our Christian faith might not in some sense be out of touch with reality and in fact completely unrealisable. Yet to pose this kind of question, or to entertain this kind of suspicion, is maybe the great temptation against which Jesus warns us in the Our Father, at the point where we pray: 'Lead us not into temptation ...'

The great temptations of life come, it would seem, curiously enough not from untruth or lies but from the truth itself. Because it is in fact true to say that our world is still imperfect. Hence if we feel downcast about the nature of our world, about the way things are and the way the world is going, we are reacting in a very understandable way to a state of affairs that we are not imagining or making up. There are in fact terrible things happening all the time in the world, and we'd only be burying our heads in the sand if we were to ignore them.

Yet for this very reason, precisely because the pain of existence is so real, we should never forget that in this life we are not dealing with nor confronted with this world only, but we are dealing with and confronted with the reality of God as well. The greatest temptation we are maybe exposed to is, therefore, not to deny or to play down, or perhaps want to justify our own imperfection or the imperfection of our world, or even to fall into despair over the general imperfection of the world and of ourselves. No. Our greatest temptation lies simply in the possibility of allowing the suffering of the world to lead us into denying or forgetting about God, or leaving him out of the reckoning altogether.

And if we succumb to this temptation, then we forget the fact that what for us is impossible can very well be possible for God, who created our world out of nothing and who through his grace can bring it to perfection, but to a perfection that can only be reached through death and resurrection, as in the case of Jesus. So, it's good perhaps to remind ourselves from time to time that our world, which often seems so final and fixed and unchanging, is in fact involved in a process of transition to a new reality, and this new reality is nothing less than the possibility that Jesus opened up for all of us to share fully in the life of God for ever and ever.

RELIGION AND MORALITY

The Advantages and Disadvantages
of Morality for Religion[1]

An idea that seems to run through all of today's three readings is that there is something more important to God, or something more important in God's eyes, than morality, or the way human beings actually behave. In the first reading, King David is confronted by the prophet Nathan with his crimes against Uriah the Hittite, whom he had arranged to have killed in battle in order to take his wife Bathsheba for himself. But for some reason, God accepts David's repentance and spares his life, even though the implication is that he really deserves to die for his crimes.

Then, in the second reading, from St Paul's Letter to the Galatians, we hear that 'no one can be justified by keeping the Law'. And that seems to imply that even if you *could* keep the Law, or even if you *could* lead a perfect, moral life, that still wouldn't win or earn you God's favour. And if we put this alongside the first reading, it looks as if the Bible is telling us that doing evil won't necessarily destroy God's love or concern for you, and doing good won't necessarily guarantee that God will show love or concern for you.

The story in the gospel reading, then, seems to take up and reinforce the message of both the first reading about King David, and also the second reading about just how far keeping the Law is likely to get us. For, in the gospel reading we see two people who seem to represent two human possibilities: on the one hand, a respectable Pharisee who takes his religion seriously and thinks of himself as an upholder of the Law, and, on the other hand, a woman 'who had a bad name in the town'. As the story unfolds, it's clear that Jesus is more taken by the woman with the bad reputation than with the respectable Pharisee. And the reason seems to be that the woman shows such more love towards Jesus than does his host, Simon the Pharisee. And interestingly, Jesus says that the woman shows such great love because she has been forgiven so much, and he adds: 'It is the man who is forgiven little who shows little love.'

Now, maybe that last remark made by Jesus was meant ironically, in the sense that no one in fact can be forgiven little, as no one in fact is without sin. So perhaps what Jesus was hinting at to Simon the Pharisee was that the woman who showed him such great love had a deeper, keener insight into her life and into her relationship with God than had Simon, for all his official interest in religion. And she may have realised more profoundly than did Simon her own dependence on God's mercy, and the precarious and hence precious nature of the reality of human life that goes with that realisation.

This is a difficult and tricky point for us to accept, I think, because the gospel seems to be saying that morality, or how we live, doesn't finally matter all that much. What really matters is realising and accepting our dependence on God and our need for his love and mercy. Now, I think we have to be careful here, because it clearly cannot be the case that morality or how we live doesn't matter. To believe that morality is of no significance would be to trivialise all the horrors of world history. It is certainly true that that precise temptation, that is to say, to see morality as unimportant, has cropped up over and over again in the history of the church,[2] when people have thought that, if they were enjoying God's favour, then it didn't matter how they lived or what they did. But this has always been seen as an aberration, not as an authentic expression of the Christian faith. So I don't think we can say that, for Christianity, morality doesn't matter. And, indeed, in recognising that the woman in the story *had* in fact sinned, Jesus is recognising the sinful nature of her actions in the past; he's not ignoring them or trying to sweep them under any carpet.

But, while we can't claim that our actions don't count for anything, we shouldn't lose sight either of even deeper matters than the question of our behaviour. These deeper matters are that we, and all of existence, have been created by God out of nothing, without any action on our own part, and we have been redeemed by the death of Christ because God judged the world to be of such value that he sent his only Son into our world of suffering and pain in order to redeem us. It's these deeper matters, over which we have no control, and which include God's mysterious, incomprehensible ability and willingness to forgive sin, that we shouldn't lose sight of or that we shouldn't let other things, such as morality – important though they undoubtedly are – distract us from or blind us to. In this sense, the woman in today's gospel story, who was at one end, the disreputable end, so to speak, of the religious spectrum was paradoxically the one who, in Jesus' view, was able to discern the nature of God more accurately than Simon, the religious professional, the pillar of the religious establishment.

Now, we shouldn't, I don't think, deduce from all this that religious establishments are bad. Far from it. It was after all the Pharisees who rescued Judaism from extinction in the first century of our era, after the Romans had destroyed Jerusalem. And without the Pharisees, Judaism may well have disappeared. But what we can deduce from today's gospel story is that religion, besides leading us to God as a guide we badly need for this purpose, can also lead us away from God. This can happen if we allow the means to become the end. Religion is a guide towards God, but a guide is only useful as a pointer to another reality. It's the reality of God that ultimately concerns us in our Christianity, and that reality is much more fundamental than the assistance religion offers us in our search for God.

GOD'S APPARENT INDIFFERENCE TO MORALITY[3]

In the first reading today, from the Book of Exodus, we heard the story of Moses' encounter with God at the burning bush, one of the most famous scenes of the Old Testament, a scene often depicted in art and commented on by various religious thinkers down the ages. When Moses asks God what his name is, all he gets by way of reply is the mysterious answer: 'I Am who I Am.' God goes on to tell Moses he is to say to the Hebrews, should they ask him: 'I Am has sent me to you.'

It's hard to make sense of either of these expressions. They seem more like a refusal to answer the question: 'Who or what is God?' And all the oceans of ink that have been spilled by different Christian writers over the centuries on these two expressions haven't succeeded in making the name or the nature of God really all that much clearer to most people. Maybe that's not something that should surprise us very much. God, we have all been told from our earliest childhood, is a mysterious God. The Old Testament says things like: 'God's ways are not our ways.' And the implication then is that we can't really be expected to understand God. His nature is beyond our comprehension. This, again, is maybe not all that surprising. When human life itself, when even the universe we find ourselves in, the concrete, visible, tangible, thoroughly perceptible universe we are part of, is so difficult to understand, despite all the advances of the natural sciences, indeed partly because of those advances, we shouldn't perhaps be too surprised to find that God the creator is mysterious also, and maybe the world and we ourselves are to that extent a reflection of the depth and mystery of God.

In more specific terms, one of the most difficult things to understand about this life is the problem Jesus alludes to in today's gospel. And that is the problem of suffering, and especially the problem of why some people seem to be the target of a blind destructive destiny, while others apparently escape almost scot-free. Why, say, in present-day Iraq, do some people get killed in random bomb explosions while others, by sheer luck it would seem, are spared. Why in the recent past in Ireland were some wiped out and others spared in all the terrible violence? And in one of the examples Jesus himself gives in today's gospel, a tower fell and killed some in Jerusalem but not others, yet only because the latter, seemingly, had the good fortune not to be in the wrong place at the wrong time. Morally, however, there appears to have been little difference between those who perished and those who escaped destruction.

What might be easier to understand, even if not to accept or endorse, would be if those who met violent deaths had done appalling things and deserved to be punished for their crimes – a question of those living by the sword also dying by it. But Christianity has always refused to acknowledge any easy correlation between the moral quality of people's lives and what happens to them as they go through life. As the New Testament puts it: 'God's rain falls and God's sun shines on good and evil alike.' It is this aspect of the way God governs the world that is very hard for us to grasp. Perhaps, however, this is something that the people of the Old Testament had a keener or more discerning insight into than we have; maybe they had a more perceptive grasp of the incomprehensibility of God's ways or of the limits of their own understanding than we do, and that may well be the reason why they eventually gave God the enigmatic name of 'I Am'.

That is to say, the people of Old Testament times realised that life is so baffling and that God is so mysterious that there is no way we can peer into his secrets or read his mind or understand his nature just from looking at what happens in the world. The world, in short, gives no infallible or unambiguous clue to the nature of God. For that reason, the only thing the Old Testament writers were prepared to say definitely about God was *that* he existed. When it came to saying *what* God was, they were a lot more reticent. Hence, in defining God as 'I Am', in *not* trying to spell out God's nature on the basis of what they knew and had experienced of this world, what the people of the Old Testament were also implying, and what Christianity subsequently has continued to believe and teach, is that God is neither tied down to nor defined by the world. This in turn suggests that, in some sense we can never penetrate, God would still be God even had he never made the world. And that means that God, who is also believed to be good and merciful, is a reality that goes beyond and is stronger than, and other than, any power in or any aspect of this world, especially any power for evil. Hence, what God plans or what he starts, he can, in principle, always bring to fruition or completion, despite all opposition.

Faith in the ultimate triumph of God's power and goodness, like the hope for the fig tree in the unpromising circumstances described in today's gospel parable, is what has sustained Christian people down through the centuries, and can still encourage us in the midst of life always to pay more attention and attach more importance to God's own reality, rather than to whatever may or may not befall us in this life.

Escaping from the Experiments of the Past[4]

The story of the Samaritan woman has gone down in history as the story of the woman who had five husbands and none. For this reason it has often become lodged in people's minds as a story about marriage. But if we listen carefully, we'll see that those parts of the story of the Samaritan woman that relate to her husbands don't seem to be at the heart of the matter in fact.

The meeting the Samaritan woman had with Jesus is only partly concerned with the woman's past. She was certainly fascinated to discover that Jesus knew so much about her. 'He told me all I have ever done,' she told her friends and neighbours. But it would be misleading to fasten upon this detail and to think the story is concerned exclusively with the question of marriage, or even that it is interested in presenting Jesus as a spooky kind of figure who had mysterious powers enabling him to look straight into people's minds and souls.

The point of the encounter is, surely, to direct the Samaritan woman's attention, and our attention too, away from the past and towards the future when God will be worshipped 'in spirit and truth'. Whatever the truth might have been about the Samaritan woman's past, or our own past for that matter, the more important truth for her and for us is to realise the destiny we all are called to in the future. Or as St Paul put it in today's second reading: '[T]hrough Jesus ... we have entered this state of grace in which we can boast about looking forward to God's glory.'

What Jesus did for the Samaritan woman was to give her a sure and a new hope for the future. And this hope put her past in perspective, in a divine perspective that liberated her from the past. Her apparently unhappy past didn't have to be an insuperable barrier to her advance towards God. And what the Samaritan woman discovered about herself and her future has proved to be true for many others ever since.

Christianity has always been about more than morality, even social morality, because it is about accepting, as the gospel today puts it in its final words, that Jesus Christ 'really is the saviour of the world'. And salvation is not about being obsessed with or stuck in the unhappiness of the past, but about looking forward to a full sharing in the glory of God in the future.

This glory of God was made visible for us all in Jesus, and it can continue to enlighten and guide our lives through time as it enlightened and guided the life of the Samaritan woman and her contemporaries 2,000 years ago.

THE POWER AND POWERLESSNESS OF RESENTMENT[5]

There could hardly be a greater contrast between any two readings from scripture than the contrast between the second reading from St Paul's first Letter to the Corinthians and the gospel reading that we have just heard. St Paul speaks about love in powerful terms that have become famous and are often quoted – they are a favourite reading at wedding masses, for example – and then in the gospel reading itself we see not, as we might expect to find in a gospel, the face of love, but the ugly face of hatred, resentment and violence. Jesus, who had acquired a high reputation as a teacher and healer in his native Galilee, entered the synagogue of his own home town of Nazareth one sabbath and began to teach. But he wasn't welcomed, as might have been expected, with open arms by the people among whom he had been brought up. Instead the unpalatable truths Jesus had to tell his fellow townsfolk provoked them to hate him and led them to want and indeed actually attempt to kill him.

This incident from early on in Jesus' public life raises an important and disconcerting question. 'Why, so often in life, does truth and goodness evoke not a response of generous acceptance from those who are exposed to it and experience it, but on the contrary provokes only their resentment and hatred and a desire to suppress it by any available means, even murder? What is disconcerting about this question is that there is, I think, no real answer to it. We might say, as with the ordinary people of Nazareth, when faced with the famous son of the town, Jesus, that a certain amount of envy can be involved. People, who have usually no problem admiring celebrities from elsewhere, often resent the fact that someone they know well and consider quite 'ordinary' should be famous because they don't see much difference between the 'ordinary' person and themselves. Hence they resent the fact that they aren't famous while the other 'ordinary' person is. This seems to be implied in the remark about Jesus: 'This is Joseph's son, surely?' That is to say, Jesus was not apparently all that remarkable a person when growing up, just the son of one of the ordinary families in the town, so: 'How dare he be famous now, when the rest of us aren't?'

Yet no matter how much we search for psychological or other reasons to explain human resentment and hatred, it still remains a mystery. In a different context, St Paul spoke of the mystery of iniquity, and that mystery of iniquity shadowed Jesus' public ministry right through to the bitter end on Calvary. Many accepted Jesus, of course, and left everything to follow him. The apostles fall into that category. But equally, Jesus provoked constantly throughout his public life, as in today's gospel, rejection, antagonism and murderous hatred for what he did and what he said, and it finally led to his crucifixion.

The gospels don't and can't and don't even try to explain in ultimate terms why this should be so, why goodness and truth should meet with both acceptance and rejection, and why in the short term it was the rejection that carried the day in the death of Jesus. The mystery of iniquity is part of the mystery of human freedom, which is finally an unfathomable and inscrutable enigma for us. But we believe that we are made in the image of God, so the mystery of our freedom must in some sense be a reflection of the mystery of God's freedom, and the good news of the gospel is that, whatever about us, God's freedom is never used for evil, but always and only for good, even if we don't and can't understand how exactly God uses his freedom and why.

The people in today's gospel reading couldn't understand either how God could act outside the parameters of the world of the chosen people of Israel in doing good, but he did. They weren't willing to trust God to do what was right, unless he did what *they* thought he should be doing. In our own day, we find ourselves in a fundamentally similar situation to the one in which the people of Jesus' day found themselves. We too have the choice between accepting goodness and truth when we are exposed to it, or trying to suppress it if it threatens our own convictions about how we think God should organise the world. But beyond our choices – and we always hope our choices will be wise and just, although they most likely won't always be – we have the good news of the gospel which assures us that God's ways always do prevail in the long run, and reveal eventually that even the power of human resentment is itself only the compliment of recognition that the mystery of iniquity pays to the mystery of goodness.[6]

CHURCH MATTERS

God and the Church[1]

We find Jesus in today's gospel, after his period of forty days in the wilderness, which we commemorate every year in the forty days of Lent, announcing the coming of the Kingdom of God. And this raises for us the old question of where this kingdom now is. Jesus came into the world as the glory of Israel and the light to enlighten the Gentiles. And Christians have always believed in Jesus as the divine person who came into the world to bring the world to salvation.

The connection between Israel and Christianity may remind us of the well-known story about the rabbi and the priest. The priest was trying to convince the rabbi that Jesus was the world's redeemer who had made human existence utterly different. The rabbi took him to the window, opened it, pointed to the world outside and asked: 'What difference do you see?' In the same way it is often said that Jesus came preaching the Kingdom of God and what came was the church, as the best-known of the early twentieth-century French modernists, Alfred Loisy, formulated the problem. Now it is undoubtedly true that the New Testament speaks about the coming of God's kingdom; and if people thought that meant that a new, perfect world was going to replace this one, they were obviously mistaken. Christians have committed all sorts of crimes down through the centuries. Christianity, for all its noble ideals, hasn't even been able to prevent Christians themselves from carrying out evil in the very name of their faith. Part of this is no doubt due to the sad truth that it appears to be nearly easier to do evil enthusiastically when you think you are doing it for God.[2] And yet, while it was a mistake to think that the Kingdom of God had replaced the old world, that mistake pointed to an important truth that remains valid for us: we are involved in a process of transition from an old world that we know only too well to a new world whose real substance we only see in a glass darkly. That transition was accomplished by Jesus and it is accessible to us as we move through our own lives. But if we want to get full access to this new world one day, then all other kingdoms and interests have to take second place; and even the church is only a pointer to God's new world. The church is not God himself.

This may seem to reduce the importance of the church, but it doesn't really. It just reminds us of the church's true nature, which is to point to the Kingdom of God, not to replace it. And even more importantly, it reminds us that the new world of the Kingdom of God is *God's* creation. We may participate in it, but we don't own it. And if it is God who brings it into being, then we shouldn't be demanding or expecting from others or indeed from ourselves what only God can give.

In our own lives here on earth we can never achieve a unity or a harmony between our existence and its meaning and value. But since we are made in God's image, we cannot but struggle to try to do so because in God there *is* such a unity. Our faith in fact teaches us, not just that we can *try* to come closer to God's kingdom in the course of our lives, but that God uses our efforts as part of the process by which he redeems us. In other words, that the turmoil and pain inseparable from human life is not in vain; indeed even our sins, we believe, can be turned by God to good account for our salvation. That's to say, even if we always fall short of the glory of God, as St Paul put it, God's providence can always be trusted to work with human faults and frailty and to bring unexpected good out of them. God doesn't necessarily have to regard sin as only something regrettable that will be punished at the Last Judgement. He can also regard sin as something from which he can extract unexpected good. Hence the ancient Christian notion of the 'happy fault of Adam that won for us so great a redeemer'.

The promise of the Kingdom of God wasn't fulfilled, then, in the way that the first followers of Jesus had anticipated; the old world wasn't replaced dramatically by a new world; paradise was not reconstituted. But the promise of the Kingdom of God, which will be mysteriously more than paradise regained, is nevertheless still valid, and the 'good news' of its reality can still guide our lives through the ambiguous and often dangerous world of human history towards the truth of the world to come.

A Church in Ruins?

Pessimists and optimists are frequently compared to those who choose to describe a half-filled glass as either half-empty or half-full. Applied to the situation of the contemporary church, the comparison might be used to describe, on the one hand, those Catholics who lament the death, or at least the severe curtailment, over approximately the last forty years of former, well-tried, cherished modes of devotion and order within the church, and their replacement by liturgical vandalism, theological glitter, and chaos; and, on the other hand, those Catholics who welcome the new dispensation as a force for liberation for both mind and body, an opportunity for rejuvenation after years, maybe even centuries, of religious stultification and suffocation. What is a 'church in ruins' for some is, for others, a church rising like a phoenix from the ashes.

The previous remarks could have been written about fifteen or twenty years ago, when debate about the state of the church was still largely an internal church matter. In the meantime, the debate has shifted. No longer is the internal life of the church a matter of heated discussion only for practising or even retired Catholics. Dark clouds now cover the church in the mind of the general public, and the activities of its clerics, above all, have become a matter of grave concern for law-enforcement agencies in many western countries, to say nothing of remaining a matter of anxiety for the higher echelons of the Catholic hierarchy, fearful of seeing whatever residual credibility the church may still enjoy in the eyes of a sceptical world vanishing completely.

Overshadowing, however, even the dark clouds of priestly sinning hovers a potentially even more intractable, even more unwelcome problem. Given that there seems to have been in the recent past – and perhaps even in earlier epochs of church history? – such flagrant discrepancy between preaching and practice, could it be not just that the church, in the persons of its officially ordained representatives, fails to practise what it preaches (a human enough predicament), but that it does not really believe in what it preaches, or at least does not have the ability or will to entertain such a possibility in order to try to remedy it? Or could it be, perhaps, that the message of Christianity has been couched in such high-minded, idealised terms that no ordinary mortal could possibly live as if he or she really believed in it as a message for this world? Being forced to deliver a message one does not – indeed, cannot – really believe in, might the messengers then perhaps settle for a double life with little or no communication between the two? Are dishonesty and hypocrisy almost inevitably pre-programmed in the church's aim of preaching the Christian gospel?

To some, such speculation may appear arbitrary or even dangerous. For who can judge another human being? Who can look into another human being's soul? Or even into one's own? It might then, perhaps, be more prudent not to 'personalise' the issues that have just been raised, but to ask simply what response, if any, can be made to the current malaise in the church. How should, how *can* one deal with a situation where a community that set out with the highest of ideals, proclaiming the good news of redemption for the whole world, has ended up being regarded as 'a church in ruins', its reputation in tatters, its message often mocked at as self-evidently phoney, its personnel mistrusted by the world at large?

One could, as a first option, simply refuse to face reality, retreat into the shadow of the ruins, and seek to defy the world and its rejection with the traditional weapons of defeat: resentment, bitterness and self-pity. Or one could take a complacent course, and say that just as a corrupt police force is better than no police force at all, or a corrupt government better than no government at all, so a corrupt church is better than no church at all. And this option may not be the least astute. But, finally, one could also attempt to see if anything can be salvaged from the shipwreck the church appears to be experiencing at the present time.

The first thing one might say in this context is that a shipwreck, despite its undeniable hardships, is not necessarily the worst fate to befall anyone. Think of Jonah (who, admittedly, was not exactly shipwrecked, but he did lose his ship when thrown overboard). Or of St Paul himself, indeed. The constant message of the Bible is that God can bring good out of evil, that he can even 'use' human evil for his own inscrutable purposes, that he can redeem human beings even from the consequences of their own sinfulness and folly. God, as the Portuguese proverb has it, writes straight on crooked lines. Thus in the Old Testament, the evil committed by his brothers against Joseph, when they sold him into slavery in Egypt, paved the way for the salvation of the Hebrew people when they were later threatened with famine in their own homeland. Or one could point to the medieval cathedrals whose ugly gargoyles, symbols of evil, were pressed into service as drains and thus compelled to fulfil a useful function by their designers.

But another equally constant message of the Bible is that when those who follow God, or think they are following God, become too snugly, even smugly, settled in their ways, disaster is rarely far off. The long habits of a religious form of life are then apt to be shattered, and those who lived by them liable to be cast out into the wilderness to seek some new 'promised land'.

In other words, the church might now possibly have the chance of learning or re-learning in practice, and not just in theory, that it does not exist for the benefit or the benefices of the clergy (humanly attractive though the latter undoubtedly are), nor even for the benefit of the whole 'people of God', but for the good of the world, as a light to the nations, and as the salt of the earth. The church, in short, is no replacement for the world, still less a substitute for God, but only a pointer to God, alas too often a negative pointer, revealing what God is not like, rather than what he is like. But even that negative theology is surely a gain.

Today, then, to return to the image used at the start, the question would no longer simply seem to be the still fairly innocent and innocuous one of some twenty years ago: is the glass half-empty or half-full? Rather the question is a more urgent and worrying one: is there any glass left at all? Is there any glass worth preserving? Presumably only God knows the answer to that question, not any church authority or any theologian. But as we believe that God is unchanging, there is every reason to believe that what he made possible in the past, he will also make possible in the future. The church, then, to conclude with another image, is less a ship than a cork, and corks are notoriously hard to sink.

HAS CHRISTIANITY BECOME MORE DIFFICULT?[3]

You sometimes hear people say that it would have been easier to be Christians, to be followers of Jesus Christ, if we had had the advantage of living 2,000 years ago and of knowing Jesus while he was on earth, or if we had had at least the advantage of hearing about him from his very first followers. People often then go on to say that it is much more difficult today to be followers of Jesus Christ, living as we do so long after the time of Jesus and so long after the first coming of the Holy Spirit at Pentecost.

Yet if we think about this notion for a while, we'll see that it only *appears* to be true, but doesn't really hold water as an idea that fully convinces. Because we know that plenty of people in fact had the advantage, as we might describe it, of seeing Jesus in the flesh, of walking and talking with him or of knowing his first followers, but that didn't persuade them to follow Jesus or to become Christians. In other words, only some of those who knew Jesus while he was on earth or heard the early preaching about Jesus believed in him, while others didn't.

And all down through the ages, right down to our own day, the same pattern repeats itself over and over again. Some who hear about Jesus Christ become his followers, while others don't. We have the opportunity of hearing about Jesus and his message through the action of the Holy Spirit in the church today, just as people had the chance of hearing about Jesus and his message in his own day, either from Jesus himself or from his followers and those who had known or heard about him. But the message is the same in both cases.

And we know from our own experience that today some choose to follow the way of Jesus and others don't, just as happened in Jesus' own time. Or perhaps, more significantly for ourselves, if we look at our own lives, we'd have to admit that sometimes we choose to try to follow Jesus, and sometimes we don't. The point is that following Jesus or not following Jesus has nothing to do with whether we were born in the first century or in the twenty-first century. The attractions *and* the difficulties of following Jesus are much the same in every age, because they are closely related to how we actually live and have to live. And the good things and the difficult things of life don't change very much from generation to generation.

I once heard of a summer course in English literature where the students were being introduced to the poetry of Milton. At the end of one of the classes, a student asked why, after all the progress the world had made since the seventeenth century, it was still necessary to be concerned with the works of a seventeenth-century writer like Milton. And the teacher replied: 'As far as I know, the death rate is still one hundred per cent.' More ruefully, Jerzy Lec observed, on this theme, that it was a pity one could only enter paradise in a hearse.[4] Now, one wouldn't want to try to frighten people into being interested in religion by constantly harping on about the reality of death, but, on the other hand, it's surely not such a bad idea to remind ourselves occasionally of the fundamental parameters within which our lives have to be lived. The beginning and the end of life is something over which we, in our own case, have no control whatsoever. That is to say, we cannot bring ourselves into existence, and we cannot prevent our existence on this earth from ending at some point in the future. The boundaries or limits of our existence here on earth cannot be eliminated or even fundamentally modified. They are unbudgeable.

At Pentecost, therefore, it is perhaps useful to call to mind once again the great truths of life and death, which, as I said, are the unchanging context within which we have to try to follow Christ. This reminds us, then, that accepting the truth and promises of Christianity is as possible – as easy or as difficult – now as it ever was in the past. But beyond that, it is also important to remind ourselves that the Holy Spirit isn't just sent to us to recall the past to our minds, and thus to help us follow Jesus, now that Jesus himself is no longer physically with us as he was in Palestine 2,000 years ago. But the Holy Spirit is also given to us to guide us into the future,[5] towards things that even Jesus himself didn't give to his first followers. Jesus said that the Holy Spirit would lead us to the 'complete truth', which implies that he left certain things still to be revealed or understood in the future.

The church, guided, we believe, through history by the Holy Spirit of God, isn't only turned towards the past, for all its incalculable significance. It is just as truly, indeed even more so, directed towards the future when we believe and hope that God will give us, after death, a share in his divine glory. This is something that is not yet fully possible for us as we travel, guided and consoled by God's spirit, through life in this world, on our way to heaven. And it is not possible for the simple reason that the created order, and even the church, of which we are a part, could no more endure full exposure to the reality of God than we could endure full and unmediated exposure to the light and heat of the sun. As the Bible puts it, man cannot look on the face of God and live.

What has Become of the Mission of the Church?[6]

Today is Mission Sunday. It's a day that was maybe easier to celebrate in former times than it is today. Not all that many years ago few, if any, doubted that it was a good and even a noble thing to join a missionary order and to dedicate one's life to spreading the Christian faith in foreign lands. Many missionaries left the country where they had been born and grown up in order to spread the faith abroad, and in lots of cases they never returned home again because travel was of course much more hazardous, laborious and expensive then than it is now. And missionaries, too, often had to endure enormous hardships, and make heroic sacrifices, even of their lives in times of persecution.

That was then, this is now. It's no secret that vocations to missionary orders – and not just to missionary orders – have fallen drastically in the church in the last number of years, in the western church anyway. While many generous people are still willing to work as lay missionaries abroad in foreign countries for a few years, not many would be willing or able to commit themselves to such a vocation for life.

The huge change that has occurred within the church in recent times with regard to the mission of spreading the faith no doubt has many causes. A major one seems to be that people have become highly sensitive nowadays to the reality of all the religious and cultural differences in the world. As a result they are hesitant about, if not downright hostile to, the idea of imposing their own views on anyone else. And in this atmosphere missionary activity is often then perceived as being aggressive and disrespectful of other people's sincerely held convictions. The word 'proselytising' has, as we know, taken on very negative overtones.

And reinforcing this negative evaluation of missionary activity has been the highlighting of the crimes committed over the centuries in the name of Christianity, by those determined to spread the faith. The negative advertising this has created for Christianity is illustrated by a chilling story told about an Indian chief in the Americas who even under the threat of death wouldn't abandon the traditional religion of his own people and accept baptism. When asked why he was so stubborn in his refusal of Christianity, he said that if he were to accept baptism and become a Christian, he would one day have to meet the God of the Christians and, given the nature of this God's followers, he preferred not to have to face that prospect.

As against such bad publicity is the frequently mentioned case of the Spanish sixteenth-century missionary friar, Bartolomé de Las Casas, who championed the cause of the Indians working in appalling conditions in gold mines in the West Indies. But even Las Casas hasn't escaped criticism. The solution to the plight of the Indians that he suggested to the Spanish Crown (while regretting it later, it would seem), and that was apparently acted upon, was that Africans should be shipped across the Atlantic to replace the Indians in the mines, as they weren't Spanish subjects, whereas the Indians were. Even philanthropy, as we see, can sometimes have sad and bizarre consequences.[7]

However, whether people take a benign or a fault-finding view of the effects of Christian missionary activity over the centuries is, I think, not really the central issue that lies behind the present-day malaise in the church about the whole idea of mission. For people, including missionaries, are only human and make mistakes, often terrible mistakes, and so the crimes committed in the name of the gospel, while infinitely regrettable, can hardly be Christianity's biggest problem on the missionary front. The deepest cause of the present malaise may be much simpler and much closer to home. It may lie in the difficulty many people have nowadays in answering honestly the simple question posed by today's gospel reading, namely: 'What does it mean to believe in Jesus Christ?' This question faces all who think of themselves, in however limited and modest a way, as Christians. And it's uncertainty about how to answer this basic, simple question that may be at the heart of the current shrinking of traditional missionary activity in the church.

But uncertainty is not necessarily a bad thing. In fact being too certain of things in religion can often turn faith into arrogance and can turn God into an idol tailored to our own wants and desires. Uncertainty in religion, on the other hand, can give us a healthy respect for God's own reality, and can make our own attempt to find God and to do God's will, a realistic enterprise rather than a piece of play-acting.

How, then, can we answer the question: 'What does it mean to believe in Jesus Christ? And how does it relate to mission?' Well, the answer to both those questions is, I think, already contained in today's gospel, if we listen to it. The faith in Jesus Christ that it highlights must involve believing that the world – despite all appearances to the contrary – is so precious in God's eyes that he wishes to redeem it for all eternity. That same faith must also involve believing that God has not only the wish but also the ability to achieve the goal of redemption. And indeed what we celebrate in the mass is precisely the redemption won by Christ's sacrifice on the cross – a sacrifice already hinted at in the strange and difficult opening lines of our first reading today from the prophet Isaiah: 'The Lord has been pleased to crush his servant with suffering … and through him what the Lord wishes will be done.'

This twofold belief in the goodness of the world God has created and in the reality of redemption has been a kind of cantus firmus, or the basic melody of Christian teaching at all times and in all places where the church has spread. And where this teaching remains audible, where it's listened to and is allowed to work itself into the fabric of our lives, then it's not all that important what other tunes happen to be in the air at any particular time, whether they are mournful or happy.

Where does all that leave mission, you might well ask. Well, mission is and always has been essential to our faith, because Christianity is not natural to us or to anyone else: no one is born with it; we have to learn it, like another language. And we can't learn it if no one teaches it to us, that is to say, if we ourselves are not 'missionised'. The good news is that all human beings, we believe, do have the capacity for learning this language. The sobering news is that no matter how well we learn it, traces of our natural language will always remain, and we will never be completely at home in the other language. Concretely, this means that, as Nietzsche put it so memorably: '[I]n reality there has been only one Christian, and he died on the Cross.'[8]

If that sounds too stark, it's really no more than what Christianity says about itself. Jesus is the only Son of God by nature; we become God's children by adoption, by the grace of baptism. And that fundamental distinction between Jesus Christ and us is presumably what is at stake in today's gospel reading, which speaks about the need to have faith in God's only Son. Strengthened by that faith we can continue to hope that the disparity we experience in this world between the music of heaven and the pain of human history will not last for ever, and we can allow our lives here on earth to be buoyed up by that hope.

Just as Christ overcame the world, so faith in Christ can do likewise. For we believe that while life may be harsh, sordid, even seemingly pointless at times, nevertheless life and we ourselves have been called into being by God – and not by ourselves – for a purpose, and God's purposes will always finally be realised. However, they will be realised in God's way, not in ours. And that is why reflection on the history of Christian missionary endeavour down the ages, instructive though it may be in many respects, is finally not what is most important. Whether the church has been as successful or as free from mistakes in the missionary task as we might ideally wish, is not what matters most. What is most important is to realise and to believe that the Christian mission isn't first and foremost about us, it's not about our going out to others with the Good News of God's kingdom, but it's about God, it's about God's mission to us, his going out to us in creating us out of nothing, and out of love for the world sacrificing his only Son to redeem us and bring us to heaven.

CHRISTIANITY AND POWER

JESUS AND THE TEMPTATIONS OF POWER[1]

It's a terrible thing, the Bible tells us, for a man to fall into the hands of the living God. But it would seem also a terrible thing for us not to recognise, or for us to misunderstand and misinterpret the living God after he allowed himself to fall into our hands in the person of his Son, Jesus Christ. But, how are we to recognise the living God in our own time and place? How are we to avoid misinterpreting the signs of his presence? How are we to prevent ourselves perhaps even from following in the footsteps of the devil in today's gospel reading, and trying to force God to reveal himself in ways that suit *us*, or trying to force God to *accept* us in return for what we think we can offer him, or finally even trying to blackmail him into doing what we want by quoting scripture against him?

The short answer to all these questions is that we can't avoid all these pitfalls. We can maybe avoid some of them some of the time, but not all of them all of the time. Whatever else Christianity means, it certainly means accepting this revelation of our human, all too human frailty as a permanent feature of our spiritual landscape. And if any spiritual maestro or theologian tries to persuade us otherwise, we have a right to be permanently sceptical towards them.

There has been no shortage of advice given in recent years to Catholics about how they should present themselves and their faith to the world of the so-called twenty-first century: recipes for renewal recommend, among other things, theological enlightenment for the people of God, in-depth biblical study, the dismantling of ecclesiastical power structures, sprightlier liturgies, the development of new Christian communities fired by an appropriate spirituality, resistance to oppression everywhere, the production of a more pastorally orientated clergy, greater concern for social, economic, political and even ecological issues. Now, whether Catholics, *qua* Catholics, have specific competence in all of these areas is unclear. But quite apart from that, the great calls for renewal have not produced a new heaven and a new earth; the magic panacea of orthopraxis has not made saints out of sinners.

If the modern renewal movement is failing to deliver the goods, running out of steam somewhat and creating much disappointment, even disillusionment, with the church, could it perhaps be because the church is a reality that cannot and should not be renewed or reformed or reshaped, because the church is at heart the mystery of Jesus Christ, the Son of God in this world, who is the same yesterday, today and for ever? St Paul writes in today's second reading: 'If your lips confess that Jesus is Lord and if you believe in your heart that God raised him from the dead, then you will be saved … That is the faith we proclaim.'

When we consider our basic attitude to the church or our role in the church, it's wrong, I think, to be concerned about any *activity* on our part at all. That's the wrong direction to look in. We must basically be *passive*. If we go back to today's gospel again, we'll see that on the three occasions the devil tempted Jesus with the offer of various types of power, he tried to get him to *do* something, but Jesus remained passive on each occasion, or to use an unfashionable word, he remained obedient, obedient to a transcendent loyalty, higher than any power in creation. In doing that he showed us what real human freedom and love are, freedom and love won through obedience or passivity. Passivity is connected with passion and passion with suffering. And suffering is the only thing in this world that doesn't cut people off from one another. It's inclusive, it draws people together, whereas action of its very nature is particular, selective and exclusive. It's hardly surprising that our redemption was won by Christ's suffering and death, which was a passion endured for the whole human race.

Christ came to seek that which was lost, that which had gone astray. Despite the relative solidity and stability of our civilizations, all human beings recognise their destiny on earth in the great symbol of exile or lostness: it's built into our myths and our prayers; *exules filii Hevae* ('poor banished children of Eve'), from the Hail Holy Queen, or the hymn 'Hail Queen of Heaven', with its phrase, 'guide of the wanderer here below'. We find it in our first reading today from the Book of Deuteronomy where Moses refers to his forefather as a 'wandering Aramaean', one of the many wanderers in the Old Testament.

Being lost, we don't always or maybe we never see clearly, but only in a glass darkly. We live by faith. Human flesh is weak; as the Lenten liturgy forcibly reminds us we are only dust, and one day will be dust again, but, to borrow words from a great seventeenth-century Spanish poet, Quevedo, we'll be dust that still can love, because we have been redeemed for ever by the love of God, incarnate in his Son, Jesus Christ.

THE TRAP OF TAXATION[2]

The reply Jesus gives in today's gospel to the Pharisees and the Herodians who were trying to trip him up with a trick question about taxes – the reply about rendering to Caesar the things that are Caesar's and to God the things that are God's – has echoed down the centuries as one of Jesus' best-known, if slightly gnomic, utterances. Whatever else it may be, it is certainly a good example of Jesus' astuteness and wisdom in dealing with his critics, showing how he was able to turn trick questions against those who posed them in order to force the questioners to think more deeply and more truthfully and more realistically about their own lives. On such occasions Jesus wasn't engaging simply in a piece of one-upmanship or trying to win a hollow victory in a battle of wits with his adversaries.

The trap that the Pharisees and the Herodians wanted to set for Jesus in today's gospel reading is clear: if Jesus said it *was* permissible to pay taxes to the Roman Emperor, he would be criticised and written off as a traitor to his own people. It's important, by the way, to remember the differences between then and now in order to get the full flavour of what was involved in the incident described. The tax in question was apparently a hated poll tax, levied for the benefit of the Roman forces of occupation in Jewish territories at the time, and frequently exacted with extreme cruelty, even sometimes under torture, whereas taxes in our world are, in principle anyway, collected in order to finance services that are for the public good. So, if Jesus had endorsed paying taxes to Caesar, the Roman Emperor, he'd have been branded as a supporter of an oppressive, foreign occupying power, and in this way his religious influence among his fellow Jews would have been severely curtailed or completely neutralised. If, on the other hand, he had recommended *withholding* the payment of taxes, he would have left himself open to being condemned as a trouble-maker and a dangerous threat to Roman rule, and in that way he could have been sidelined by the political establishment of the day. Either way, he would have been outmanoeuvred by his opponents and would have probably lost all credibility.

Jesus' way of avoiding the trap set for him is to turn the question against the questioners by asking to see 'the money [they] pay the tax with'. The fact that they carry such money with them shows that they have already answered the question at issue in their own lives, that is to say, they have accepted the reality of Roman rule with all the benefits and drawbacks that would entail. Hence, they don't really need Jesus to tell them what they have already decided to do anyway. In this sense, Jesus' technique is reminiscent of his advice to those who criticise others, to take the beam out of their own eye first, before trying to remove the speck from other people's eyes, or his ironic invitation to whose who are without sin to cast the first stone.

But today's encounter between Jesus and the Pharisees and the Herodians isn't just about showing Jesus' cleverness in dealing with hypocritical and sly opponents. It has a much deeper significance. Because when Jesus asks whose image is on the coin, and is told it is the image of the Roman emperor – who was depicted as a *god* on such coins – both he and his opponents would have seen at once the implication of such a question and such a reply. As Jews they would all have believed that there is only one God, and hence that the image of the allegedly divine Roman Emperor was from a Jewish point of view blasphemous. And furthermore, for Jews, as for Christians, the only image of God acknowledged by the Bible is the image of God present in all human beings. So, Jesus forces his opponents to question what image of God they truly believe in: the dead, even if shiny and glittering, image of money and worldly power, so often used to oppress and enslave people, or the image of God in themselves and others, which is alive and indestructible, reflective of God's creative and living goodness, a goodness that – unlike the empires and stock markets of this world – will never collapse.

Jesus is not chiefly concerned with pointing out 'the limits of state power'.[3] He isn't laying down hard and fast rules about church–state relations or about how religion and politics should or might be related. Times and circumstances change and people have to work out in their different societies what is the emperor's and what is God's. But the real validity of Jesus' guidance remains intact through all the vicissitudes of history: namely that the value of human existence doesn't depend on anything in this world, on any visible greatness or recognition, although such things may reflect it; rather the value of human existence depends solely on the living God in whose image we have all been created.

JESUS AND THE REALITY OF POWER[4]

Today we celebrate the Solemnity of Christ the King, the last Sunday in the Liturgical Year. Usually, in the last Sundays of the year, the church directs our attention towards the end of the world, the end of time. That was the case in the readings last Sunday. This Sunday the gospel reading, at any rate, contains no specific mention of the end of the world or the end of time, but it does talk directly about the kingship of Jesus.

It is frequently said that notions of kingship don't mean much to people nowadays, because whatever kings are left in the world have a mainly ceremonial or representational role to play in the lives of their different countries, whereas in the days of Jesus and his first followers, kings were still politically and militarily powerful and very significant figures. That is, I'm sure, true, but yet no matter how much times have changed since the days of Jesus, the world is still full of powerful political and military leaders whose behaviour has enormous influence on the lives of other people. These leaders may not call themselves 'kings' any more, but the enormous power they wield is still real enough.

And it's in the context of this kind of power – the power that can literally decide the life and death of innumerable people – that we have to try to understand what is meant by the kingship of Christ, the Solemnity we are celebrating today. Very often people maintain that religion shouldn't be involved in worldly affairs, politics in particular, but that it should be about people's relationship with God, and about heavenly matters only. Yet we see the central figure of our religion, Jesus Christ, right in the middle of politics and political power, being questioned by a powerful political figure, Pilate, the Roman governor of Judaea, about matters of such practical, down-to-earth, political importance that they eventually lead to his death. Pilate, like all rulers, is interested in power and in the status and security he thinks it gives him, and that's why he cannot but be interested in someone like Jesus who seemed to exercise a great hold over people. Pilate, at the end of Jesus' life, just like King Herod at the start of Jesus' life, was worried about Jesus. People like Jesus, who attract large numbers of followers, even if they've no interest in exercising political power, are inevitably a political force to be reckoned with in the eyes of those who hold political power and are afraid of losing it.

But Pilate doesn't seem to have understood the difference Jesus was trying to get him to see and appreciate between the kind of power that he, Pilate, exercised and the kind of power that Jesus was interested in. Jesus was talking about the power of truth, which doesn't need to be exercised, simply recognised, acknowledged and respected, because it is the reality of God himself. We can either 'listen to' this truth, as Jesus says in his conversation with Pilate, or we can ignore it. And listening to God's truth is not about trying to perceive or understand some very difficult and obscure mystery beyond this world and beyond this life. It's about how we live in the obscurity of *this* world, where the demands of truth will always make themselves heard and felt, even if we don't always see clearly what the ultimate source or the ultimate goal or end of truth is.

But there are countless occasions in human life when we are faced with choices between doing what we know is right and true, and betraying our consciousness and awareness of what is right and true. That's why Jesus never speaks about escaping from the demands of this world or never invites his followers to escape from this world into another one. Rather he speaks about being born and coming into the world precisely for the purpose of bearing witness to the truth in the here and now, in *this* world. The power he represented, the power of truth, the power and reality of God – that power made him a king, but a king of a different kind from the kings and rulers of this world. His crown wasn't a crown of jewels but a crown of thorns. He didn't take his seat on a throne of gold or sapphire, but was finally nailed to a cross. The cross was *his* throne, the price he paid for being the truth in a world of corruption and lies. Jesus' kingship represents the reversal of the normal values we find in this world, and to which we're all, I think, inclined to pay *some* homage at least. Why, otherwise, are we so interested in the lives of the powerful and rich and famous?

Such interest is perhaps natural and human, and not entirely misguided, because our faith tells us that we are made for a great destiny, that we are made for life with God. But our Christian faith reminds us in the final days of the church's year that the ultimate things, the last things, the things that really matter here on earth, the things that will finally endure, the things that are ultimately real and true, are not political or military or economic power for their own sake, but the reality of God himself who revealed his truth to the world in Jesus Christ. This is a truth that is different from any purely human, self-assertive power; it is a truth that human power can certainly *try* to destroy and eliminate and suppress, but it will never succeed in destroying or eliminating or suppressing it, because the power and reality of truth, like Jesus, will always finally rise triumphant from the dead.

DEATH AND ETERNAL LIFE

Religion and Death[1]

Gore Vidal, a keen and incorruptible observer of the religious scene, in his celebrated 'historical novel', *Julian*, has the fourth-century pagan rhetorician, Libanius of Antioch, say about the Christians:

> What most disturbs me is their curious hopelessness about *this* life, and the undue emphasis they put on the next. Of course eternity is larger than the brief span of man's life, but to live entirely within the idea of eternity is limiting to the spirit and makes man wretched in his day-to-day existence, since his eye must always be fixed not on this lovely world but on that dark door through which he must one day pass.[2]

Libanius' views reflect an enduring perception of Christianity as other-worldly and consequently life-denying; in short, as being more concerned with death than with life.

It is surely not without irony that a religion which began by declaring that death had lost its sting should eventually come to be perceived as having put the sting back into death, poisoning all of life's pleasures. Yet such a perception oversimplifies the subtle dialectic between the attachment to life and the knowledge of death that characterises human existence. This permanent dialectic can breed both resentment towards an existence which must end, and also, by contrast, a desire for immortality, for an everlasting connection with the eternal spring of life. Poised ironically between these two extremes is Proust's idea that death 'cures us of the desire for immortality'.[3] Even more curious, however, is the seeming collusion between death and what it destroys. For death's ever-present threat appears also to be the condition of life's peculiar beauty. 'Life's greatest charm is borrowed from death; it is only beautiful because it is transitory,' wrote Friedrich Hebbel,[4] a sentiment often echoed in modern times, most memorably perhaps by Wallace Stevens ('Death is the mother of beauty'). Rather than being perceived as the narrow gate leading to eternity, death, or rather the thought of death, is felt – particularly by moderns – as the spice giving life its unique savour.

Where, one could well ask, does that leave the relationship between death and religion now? Certainly, the dominant, modern sensibility or *Lebensgefühl* is a far cry from the centuries-old 'Platonic sense of life' that viewed the beautiful on earth as simply a reflection of eternal beauty, not its exhaustive incarnation. The weakening of the Platonist legacy, which was in the past eagerly exploited as a vehicle for Christian eschatology, may mark then the death-knell of Christianity's grip on the western imagination. Or it may simply be that one way in which Christianity conceived the link between time and eternity has come to an end. But death, religion's most faithful ally, still continues poker-faced to point towards eternity and, paradoxically, to enhance and undermine the securities of time.

THE FEAR OF GOD[5]

Today is the start of the season of Advent, the beginning of the period of the year when the church encourages us to concentrate once again on the saving truth of God's advent or arrival into our world at the Incarnation.

And yet the gospel we've just heard alerts us not to the imminence of some wonderful event we should rejoice over, but appears to be warning us about the impending arrival of some kind of disaster or cataclysm, and urging us to stay awake so as not to be caught unawares by what might be about to happen. That seems a far cry from what we might have expected to hear on this first Sunday of Advent. So why this unusually grim opening gospel for the beginning of Advent? And indeed, why does the whole tone of Advent with the use of solemn, not to say sombre, vestments, and the omission of the Gloria in the mass seem subdued and, if today's gospel is anything to go by, even somewhat disquieting? Why, on this first Sunday of Advent at least, does the church seem to have deliberately picked a gospel calculated to create a mood of foreboding and unease, rather than one of joyful expectation?

One reason for this that might be given is to say that looking forward to the approach of God must involve more than simply preparing to commemorate Christ's birthday once again. If we are serious about waiting for God, if talk of the approach of God is to be realistic, and not just a distraction from the rush or even the boredom of the daily round, then the reality of God has somehow got to cut through the normal routine of our everyday world, because God is more than the normal routine of that world. But in the normal run of things, most people, even professional 'religious' people, cannot take much note of God in any sustained way, because they are genuinely too preoccupied with the business of living. So perhaps that's why the images used in today's gospel are violent and, in their randomness, even cruel. For as such, they have the power to shock and make us sit up and take notice. But take notice of what? Is the violent imagery of today's gospel just a rhetorical trick for focusing our attention on ultimate human questions? Or is there perhaps also something genuinely foreboding and threatening about God and about the prospect of meeting God face to face?

In general, Christianity has, I think, tried to avoid giving any simplistic answer to this question. On the one hand, we have been told that God is love, and hence attractive to human beings. On the other hand we have been told that life is real, not an illusion, and that we will be held accountable by God for our actions – and *that*, understandably, tends to introduce an element of uncertainty and even fear into religion, despite all assertions about genuine love casting out fear. There doesn't seem to be any way that we have of finally resolving the difference between these two conflicting sides of our picture of God within the confines of this world. Which is perhaps why Christianity has traditionally seen death as the privileged agent of religion. In death – we have been encouraged to believe – God's definitive advent or coming to us personally is going to occur, and put an end to the general invisibility of God in the world, and put an end also to our own uncertainty about how we really stand in God's eyes. In this perspective, however, actually *living* in this world seems a bit like listening to an orchestra tuning up its instruments before the start of a concert, without the concert ever beginning.

This traditional Christian view of the human condition adds up to a vision of existence that would probably not be described as too rosy.

And yet this world, we believe, is God's creation, and the gospel, the church tells us, is God's good news for the world. So the good news must be something that is not unaware of life's harsh realities and its final extinction in death, but nevertheless still finds it worthwhile to believe and hope in God and to believe in the value of this incomplete and ambiguous life we have here on earth. That, of course, still leaves open the question of what exactly we value in life, what exactly we are looking for in life, and how this relates, if at all, to God. In the season of Advent, the church, in trying to shake us out of our usual spiritual torpor, suggests an answer to these questions – not, however, by directing our attention to what we should be doing about God, but rather reminding us of what God has done and will do for us. Now, it's undeniable that God's advent has usually been associated with the moment of death in Catholic culture, but surely what the Catholic faith was trying to articulate with its emphasis on death is that the certainty of God's advent to us is as real as the certainty of death itself. And the God we believe we are going to meet unambiguously in death is the same God who became incarnate in Jesus Christ. And that is good news.

But Advent is also the time when we are reminded that God *first* meets us, as the Incarnation shows, in life, not in death. In itself, death has no meaning. Any meaning it has, it derives entirely from life. But only if we find in life at least some hint of what we would want to enjoy for ever will *eternity* seem desirable. Our faith teaches us that what ultimately gives life its savour is not our love for God but God's love for the world. That love became incarnate in Jesus Christ who took away the sins of the world and made a share in divine glory possible for us. But that glory was bought at a huge price, the death of God himself. Hence, it is only fitting that in giving thanks to God, which we do in every mass, we don't ignore or play down or try to eradicate this perplexing side of our salvation. The season of Advent – with its restrained sense of what is at stake in human existence – was always meant, I think, to underline this aspect of our redemption. And we too, in accepting the fact that this world is not yet paradise, in enduring the perennial shortcomings and frustrations of existence, can echo in some faint way the sacrifice Christ made for our salvation and thus prepare ourselves to share one day in its fullness.

ON NOTHING[6]

A famous sonnet by the seventeenth-century Spanish poet Góngora, on the instability and inevitable decay of all human life, even the most beautiful, ends with an unforgettable evocation of the actual process of final human disintegration: 'into earth, smoke, dust, shadow, nothingness' (*'en tierra, en humo, en polvo, en sombra, en nada'*). The 'extraordinary falling cadence' (Arthur Terry) of this line, mirroring the transformation of human life on its final journey into annihilation, is clearly echoed at the end of the century by the last great poetic figure of the Spanish 'Golden Age', Sor Juana Inés de la Cruz, one of whose sonnets, describing a flattering portrait, ends with the memorable line: 'it is a corpse, it is dust, it is shadow, it is nothing' (*'es cadáver, es polvo, es sombra, es nada'*).

Moving, even thrilling, though such images of human extinction, and of its inexorability, can undoubtedly be, they do also, by their sheer beauty, seem to undermine the straightforward message they appear to enunciate so definitively. It is almost as if language itself were incapable of encapsulating or incarnating fully convincingly the notion of 'nothing'; even the idea of 'nothing', a moment's reflection tells us, is itself 'something', and hence is itself a contradiction of the very thing that thought is trying to conceptualise. In this case, therefore, both poetic imagination and prosaic analysis coincide in suggesting the, at best, precarious status of the concept of 'nothing', if not its outright meaninglessness.

Language's 'happy fault' in this respect, its failure to be able to conceive of 'nothing', may, for some perhaps, be an indication of the unfortunately ineluctable reality of existence, the indestructibility of what Schopenhauer called the 'will to life'. For others, the same fault will be seen to support rather than to subvert religion's sense not just of the ontological superiority of life over death, or (more abstractly) of being over nothingness, but also of life's inevitable, ultimate victory over death. Thus, even the baroque pessimism in which, for Sor Juana, the high hopes of Renaissance humanism were finally buried, can, in its sombre beauty, be viewed dialectically as an affirmation of the pull of eternity.

BEYOND DEATH[7]

It's very difficult to speak about death because there is nothing else quite like it. In fact the only comparison you can find or make for death is with the whole of life itself. In one of Victor Hugo's poems – if my memory serves me right – he made the striking remark that when a person dies, the whole universe is decapitated. No single one of us is, of course, the centre of the universe, but when each one of us dies, a particular way of looking at and experiencing the world that was unique to us will cease. What Tomás Ó Criomhthain wrote about his own people of the Great Blasket island applies, for those who are willing and perceptive enough to see it, to all human beings: '… the like of us will never be again.'

For the living who suffer the death of someone they love there is no ritual, no explanation, no consolation that can dissolve the mystery of loss and restore the status quo, because the one who died was unique, and after their death life can and will never be the same again.

We all know this, people have known it from the dawn of history, and yet we still haven't got used to it, even when and maybe especially when we make death a taboo subject. It just doesn't seem fair that this miracle of life and the people we know and love in it should be taken away from us; it seems even less fair that life is often taken away from people in the most brutal, inhuman, murderous and degrading ways. Human beings instinctively ask: 'Why must the gift of life end up for so many in unspeakable misery and squalid death, and for all of us in some form of death?' Job can stand here as a symbol of the human refusal to sweep such questions under the carpet or to be browbeaten by pious bullying into not asking them.

But the fact that we instinctively and continually rebel against the idea that injustice and death should have the last word about life is a hint to us that the way we experience reality here and now is not the way reality will ultimately be. Here on earth we are not what we will finally be, even though what we will finally be we don't yet know, since – as St John wrote – it has not yet been revealed to us.

We live by faith, which, if it is genuine, can take ignorance about the ways of God in its stride. Our faith tells us that injustice and death do not have the last word about life, just as they didn't have the first one either. In the beginning was not injustice and death, nor even the world itself, but in the beginning was the Word through whom the world was made and who in Jesus Christ became the world's Redeemer. Job's faith in a living Redeemer was vindicated in Jesus Christ in whom, as St Paul in today's second reading spelt out for us, God's love is active towards us in a way that nothing can ever undermine.

Thinking and brooding about death and its undoubted terrors can, however, sometimes induce us to be more concerned with what Christ has saved us from here on earth than with the glory that his victory over death in the resurrection has made possible for us. In this world, we should perhaps remind ourselves from time to time, we are only being prepared for heaven, even though of course without this world we would never get to heaven. Our faith in God teaches us that what matters most here on earth is not the experience we may think we have or don't have of God in the face of death, but the experience God has of us. Experience in its root meaning is concerned with testing and trying. God's experience of us is the testing we must go through in order to reach heaven. If we have faith in God, any pain we have to suffer in life can be outreached by the joy of knowing that our lives, painful and finite though they are, are being tested by God and hence are in God's hands. That is the secret of true religious peace, and likewise the liberating truth and relief of tragedy, for tragedy always brings us up sharply against the limits of our human condition and in so doing allows us painfully to learn something of the power that set those limits and thus created meaning for our world.

We moderns seem sometimes more keen to want to experience and thus test God than to allow ourselves to be tested and experienced by God. In trying to take religion seriously in this way, in making ourselves responsible for it, we confuse our role with God's and the result can't but be slightly ridiculous. Bishops worry about their pastoral responsibilities; priests worry about running their parishes; theologians worry about their relevance. Could this ever be the case, if we really believed our redemption was an accomplished fact that no worldly power could ever undo? A religion with human beings and their problems at centre stage is not true religion; at least it's not true Christianity.

It is interesting to look back sometimes at our forbears in the faith and see how they responded to the great truths of Christianity.

> We possess a Ritual from Besançon for the year 1582 which gives the following directions for Vespers on [Easter Sunday] 'After the ending of None the dances take place in the cloisters, or if the weather is wet, in the centre of the nave. During these are to be sung the chants found in the processional. And when the dance is ended drinks of red and white wine will be served in the chapter house.' We possess an even more exact account of this Easter custom in the case of the cathedral of Auxerre. There the dance, combined with a sacral ball game, took place in the cathedral choir and ... upon the so-called 'labyrinth' which decorated the floor in the form of a mosaic ... To the melody and rhythm of the Easter sequence, *Victimae paschali*, bishop and clerks moved in a carefully regulated dance order over the pattern of the labyrinth, throwing ... the Easter ball to one another, rejoicing like children in their redemption, for this was the evening of the day which had celebrated the victorious sun of Easter.[8]

We may smile or even laugh at such practices. They may strike us nowadays as childish or mind-boggling or not serious enough in religion. But surely they're the practices of people who believed that God and the redemption won for them by God in Christ were at the centre of religion, and they rejoiced in this fact. They're not the practices of people taking the weight of the world's problems on their shoulders, but the practices of people who find Christ's burden light and his yoke easy.

We of course are not sixteenth-century people, but the faith we have inherited from our forbears mustn't be allowed to be weighed down and choked by the cares and anxieties of this world. It must be what it has fundamentally been down through the centuries: a joyful act of thanksgiving to God who has called us out of nothingness into being and who – even beyond death – offers us and all the faithful departed a share in everlasting glory.

DEATH AND THE REALITY OF GOD[9]

The message in today's gospel reading is clear. It is telling us to be alert, to be vigilant, to be always prepared. Now, we might well ask, prepared for what? Traditionally, this has been answered by saying that we should be ready for the hour of death, when we have to leave this world and face our Maker. The coming of the Son of Man, in other words, has usually been interpreted as being, or coinciding with, the moment of death, as if that were the key moment in our lives for which we should always be ready and waiting.

An illustration of the importance the moment of death definitely acquired in Christian culture can be seen in one of the most frequently recited Catholic prayers, the Hail Mary, which, as we know, ends by invoking Mary, the Mother of God, and asking her to 'pray for us sinners, now and at the hour of our death'. Now, whether the huge religious and existential significance, which the moment of death has been invested with in our culture, is necessarily a good thing or not is certainly a legitimate question. An even more important question is whether the reality of death or indeed the very moment of death was ever actually intended by Christianity to have the kind of significance it came to take on?

Some of what Jesus said should perhaps make us doubt that this was what the Christian faith really intended. Jesus seems, for instance, to have been much more concerned with the death of the soul than with the death of the body. Warning about the approach of death doesn't appear to have been a very prominent part of his teaching at all. But, for example, he did say that we shouldn't worry too much about what can kill the body; rather we should worry about what can kill the soul. On another occasion, he said that we know we have passed from death to life if we love, rather than hate. On yet another occasion, he said that eternal life was to know God and the One God had sent. We don't, in other words, have to wait for death in order to know and love God. Even more importantly, we don't have to make an idol out of death, and put it on a par with God. As Oscar Wilde wrote: 'Death is not a god. He is only the servant of the gods.'

Now, we might say that that is all fine and true, but is it a truth we can experience here and now? How many people can honestly say that they are so at one with God that death has no more meaning for them? That, as St Paul said, whether we live or whether we die, we belong to the Lord? Well, some can, and some have. They are the great saints of the church who in their lives have experienced what they sometimes describe as union with God. But to achieve such union with God, they also speak about giving up everything else, dying to themselves, dying to their own will, and accepting the ultimate reality of God's will alone. Even in the garden of Gethsemane, before the crucifixion, Jesus himself wanted to have the chalice of suffering pass him by, but in the end he abandoned his own will, died to it, and accepted the will of his Father, and thus brought the human race to redemption. Of course, not all of us will be able to attain the heights of self-denial reached by the great saints, but we can at least try to keep moving in that direction.

However, over and above all that, we can take comfort from the deepest truth of our religion, which is hinted at in the final words of today's gospel, when Jesus says: 'You also must be prepared, for at an hour you do not expect, the Son of Man will come.' This statement, if we think about it, contains a very consoling thought. For, if we don't become obsessed with the actual time of the Son of God's coming to us, traditionally associated with the hour of our death, but concentrate rather on the promise Christ made to us that he *would* come to us, then we'll see that the most important reality in our religion is not whether we will be fully ready for God or not, when he comes, but to believe in the promise God made to us that he *would* come. In short, the faith that matters most isn't our faith in God, but it is rather God's faith in us. For all its sin and horror, the world has been found by God to be worth dying for. In that sense, God has faith in us. This is the good news of Christianity, and it shouldn't be confused with any other kind of news, however exalted and momentous.

The Point of the Ascension[10]

Today we celebrate the feast of the Ascension of Our Lord into heaven. Our first reading tells us that Jesus appeared to his disciples for forty days after his resurrection and then ascended into heaven, leaving the disciples somewhat at a loss about what to do next. From our vantage point, we know that the disciples received the Holy Spirit at Pentecost and went out into the whole world to preach and teach all the nations about Jesus, and to baptise all those who received the good news in the name of the Father and of the Son and of the Holy Spirit. The disciples, with the guidance of the Holy Spirit, brought the church into being and it has been spreading throughout the world ever since, right down to our own day.

However, it's still important for us today to look back to the Ascension of Our Lord and to remind ourselves about what it means for us. Of course it signalled the beginning of the work of the church in history, but it also indicates to us what the church is engaged in and what destiny the church holds out in prospect for all of us. It's important for us to remember always that Jesus did not only rise from the dead. That is the mystery of the resurrection that we celebrate in this Easter season. But just as important for us is to realise what happened or what Jesus did when he rose from the dead, never to die again. Perhaps to see what's really involved here, it might be better to ask: 'For what purpose did Jesus rise from the dead?'

And that's what the feast of the Ascension can tell us. Because today's feast tells us that Jesus rose from the dead in order to return to his Father in heaven. And we too hope to rise from the dead, not just so as to be able to say we have survived death, but in order to reach heaven and to be with God and to live the fullness of life with God and all his saints and all our relations and friends who have gone before us into eternity.

In other words, it's why we want to rise from the dead that should really concern us, not just whether we are going to survive death or not. St Ambrose said at the burial of his brother that eternal life would be just a weariness – or, we might say, 'a bore' – if it were not transfigured by grace. Perhaps this is what Nietzsche, in his incomparably provocative way, was hinting at when he contrasted 'eternal life' with *'eternal liveliness'*.[11] Rather more sedately, Christianity has traditionally contrasted nature with grace, and taught that our existence on earth (nature) is made possible by God, and is created in view of everlasting enjoyment of the glory of God, this process being nurtured on earth by the movements of divine grace.

Yet it would be disingenuous to ignore the fact that in modern times the link or connection between this earthly process and, for Christian faith, its final glorious denouement in heaven has become not so much weakened or difficult to perceive, but has rather been rejected, not to say resented, as a pernicious threat to the authentic living of earthly life. The hope of heaven is often seen as undermining the possibility of living life with maximum honesty and intensity. The Nietzsche admirer and commentator, Walter Kaufmann, may be taken as exemplary in this regard. In *The Faith of a Heretic*, he writes unapologetically: 'The life I want is a life I could not endure in eternity. It is a life of love and intensity, suffering and creation, that makes life worth while and death welcome. There is no other life I should prefer. Neither should I like not to die.'[12]

This is no doubt a salutary warning about the dangers of speaking too glibly or too thoughtlessly about eternal life. And it might help us to realise – fittingly, on a feast such as today's – that what most concerns us about eternal life, or at least what ought to concern us most about eternal life, from Christianity's point of view, is the *quality* of that eternal life; not whether there is an eternal life, but rather whether our eternity is going to be a life of joy and happiness with God and each other, or an eternity of gloom and despondency. And this is what the often contentious church teaching about heaven and hell is perhaps trying to get us to see.

Not everyone of course agrees with Christian faith on this particular point. Quite apart from modern thinkers, like Walter Kaufmann, who find any idea of eternal life – heaven or hell – not only irrelevant or meaningless but potentially inimical to the business of living *this* life, one could point to the very *sui generis* attitude to the possibility of hell of the Spanish religious thinker, Miguel de Unamuno, who wrote that he would rather spend eternity in hell than cease to exist altogether. That is certainly an unusual and, if not life-affirming, at least self-affirming, point of view, and, interestingly enough, different from both orthodox Christianity and the convictions of a thinker like Walter Kaufmann, at least in formulation.

But traditionally Christianity has taught that the deepest truth is not simply the fact of our own existence or our own creation, but rather God himself, and the belief that God wishes to share his life with us. Hence the importance of today's feast. It is not just a reinforcement of the feast of the resurrection, which celebrates Jesus' rising from the dead, but it is a feast that celebrates the reason for wanting to rise from the dead or that celebrates the whole point of rising from the dead, which for Christian faith is the sharing in God's own life for all eternity.

Jesus has gone on in the Ascension to prepare a place of happiness for all of us, not just beyond death but in the fullness of God's kingdom in heaven, which we hope will be our final goal one day too.

THE ASSUMPTION OF MARY[13]

Today we celebrate the feast of the Assumption of Mary into heaven. What this feast proclaims is that Mary was taken up, body and soul, into heaven, when her earthly life had ended. And when we ask if that means anything specifically for us, or if it concerns Mary alone, then we can say that it means everything to us, because what Mary now enjoys in heaven by the special grace of God is what is promised to all of us by God at the end of the world.

We, too, are offered the same destiny that Mary reached on being taken up into heaven. As we go through life, the promise of a glorious destiny is something that can comfort and encourage us, especially in the dark days and the difficult times that every human life experiences.

There is, however, another important side to today's celebration that we shouldn't lose sight of: our destiny is not just to save our souls but to live with God and with one another, body and soul, in heaven. In other words, our bodies are as much a part of us as our souls, not just some kind of container or piece of luggage that contains the real 'us'. The English language, I think, indicates this in the way it sometimes uses terms like 'somebody', 'anybody', or 'nobody', in referring to human beings.

Now if we are asked, 'Why is it so important to insist on our bodies as well as on our souls?' we can say that if we want to get to know the true God, and to appreciate his creation as he intended it we must insist on both. There is always and always has been a great temptation to see the world of creation, the visible, material world as somehow not quite real, or even as something evil in itself. This temptation arises, understandably enough, because of the physical sufferings people often have to endure and because all life ends, in the short term at any rate, in death and in the dissolution of the body. Nothing, then, is easier in these circumstances than to say: 'The material, visible, physical world is ultimately unimportant, is even perhaps intrinsically evil, the spiritual or intellectual world alone is good and God-like. Hence the body is unimportant, and only the soul matters.' But our faith tells us: No. All creation comes from God, and in our case both our body and our soul are created by God. As we proclaim in the Creed: God is the creator of everything visible and invisible. The creation is marred and distorted by sin. That is undeniable, but it is still God's creation and it is still fundamentally good, both in its material and in its spiritual dimensions. What's more, if the spiritual creation was all that really mattered, then God the Son would not have had to be born of Mary, whose Assumption into heaven, body and soul, we are celebrating today. In other words, if the Word had been enough, then the Word would not have had to become flesh.

The importance of the body as well as the soul is also the deepest reason why we are encouraged to respect God's creation and the life within it, why Jesus encouraged us to clothe the naked, feed the hungry, shelter the homeless, visit those in prison, to do all the other 'corporal' works of mercy. And that's also why the church identifies the weakest and most vulnerable physical moments of human life –

before birth and before death – as worthy of special care and attention. But all that only underlines the value at all times of all human life, made in the image of God. The material world wasn't a mistake God made.

Today's feast of the Assumption has profound meaning for us, and above all reminds us that we didn't make this world, with its specific laws and structures and form, nor did we make ourselves with our bodies and our souls. We are born into this world, body and soul, and we have to try to discover God's plan for us, as incarnate spirits, not pure spirits, as we go through life, rather than wanting to impose on God our plans, or our ideas of how we think the world should have been made. Mary, the Mother of God, is a reliable guide for us in this faith because she accepted fully the reality of God's creation, and, as today's feast of the Assumption proclaims, the path she followed brought her to the full reality of her human destiny and to a share in God's glory in heaven. We too can all look forward to sharing in this one day, if we try to follow Mary's example and to find our way to heaven in and through the world that God has created for us and in which he has placed us, body and soul.

Aspects of the
History of
Christianity

CHRISTIANITY AND HELLENISM[1]

Horace's celebrated remark, *'Grecia capta ferum victorem cepit'* ('Greece, once captured, took her barbarous captor captive'), was made in relation to the influence of Greek culture (especially poetry) on the civilization of Rome. Rome had come to dominate Greece militarily in the second century BC and had absorbed the country into its own political sphere of influence, making it a Roman province. But culturally Greece's influence on Rome was vast, especially in the fields of philosophy and literature. Hence Horace's famous dictum. But a surely weightier historical irony occurred in the centuries after Horace (65–08 BC) when, in the shape of Christianity, a small Jewish sect infiltrated the Graeco-Roman world and eventually came to dominate it. This is acknowledged even by those, like Gibbon (who saw the Christian conquest of the Roman Empire as 'the triumph of barbarism and religion') and Nietzsche ('Christianity robbed us of the harvest of the ancient world'), who, in different measures, abhorred this triumph as one of the great disasters to befall humanity.

At the time of the origins of Christianity, the Graeco-Roman world was, culturally, Hellenistic. Earlier, in the fourth century BC, the sweeping conquests of Alexander the Great had overwhelmed the Jewish heartland of Palestine, as well as engulfing such significant centres of the Jewish diaspora as Egypt (the still extant Egyptian city of Alexandria is evidence of Alexander's superb megalomania). The sustained policy of fostering a Hellenistic style of life among the conquered peoples who found themselves in the new empires to emerge in the immediate aftermath of Alexander's death was hugely successful, even in the case of Judaism. Indeed, the Septuagint, or Greek translation of the Hebrew Scriptures made in Egypt in the third and second centuries BC, could serve as an inestimably significant example of how irresistibly attractive the new international arrangements proved to be. Yet the attempt to foist Hellenistic values on Jews did eventually meet with some serious resistance, as demonstrated by the Maccabean wars of the second century BC, when traditional elements within Judaism challenged the ascendancy of foreign ways, perceived as anti-religious from a Jewish perspective, and sought to defend their ancestral faith from the threat of extinction.

The Maccabean struggle succeeded in establishing a short-lived Jewish state that was finally destroyed by the Roman general Pompey in 63 BC. But in the following century, another Jewish movement, this time with no military dimension, set out, using the weapons of the conquerors – their language (the New Testament was written in Greek) and their more visible means of communication in the shape of their roads – and perpetrated what might be described as a belated, but long-lasting act of revenge on the mighty conquerors of former times.

If nothing else, the rise of Christianity does indeed seem to support the idea that the pen is mightier than the sword, or, in more traditionally religious language, that the spirit is more durable, and perhaps also more cunning, than even any political power.

CHRISTIANITY AND ANTI-SEMITISM[2]

Matricide is an awe-inspiring crime. To kill another human being is vile enough, to kill one's own mother, to deprive of life the person who gave one life, is to move into a different dimension of horror. It represents an almost metaphysical assault on the very order of reality. Yet, if scholars are correct who tell us that Christianity sprang from Judaism, then Christian anti-Semitism, which has frequently in the course of history not stopped short of murder, could be interpreted as a form of matricide, of religious or, at least, religiously inspired matricide.

That religion should inspire murder is, of course, nothing new. Indeed the first recorded murder in the Bible has a specifically religious dimension. Cain killed Abel, we are told, out of envy: Abel and his offerings found favour with God, whereas Cain and his offerings didn't (cf. Gen 4:3-5). Yet making all due allowances for the power of envy and other unlovely human passions, it is still quite puzzling to be confronted with a religion teaching love even of one's enemies, veering off eventually into matricide. Perhaps the question of identity might provide a clue to illuminate this murky mystery.

While many will commit crime for fear of poverty, psychologists assure us that the most insidiously dangerous kind of poverty is to be deprived of one's identity. It is often claimed that the recent, and perhaps still unfinished, conflict in Northern Ireland is about the protagonists' sense of their own identity rather than simply a sordid squabble over land and power. Or rather, the latter, while real, is only the expression of a deeper need. It is only the means by which a deeper need can be satisfied: the need to preserve and reinforce the identity one would like to coincide with and parade before the world.

What has any of this to do with Christian anti-Semitism? In all likelihood, quite a lot. According to its own self-understanding, Christianity is not merely the fulfilment of Judaism, but Judaism should have transformed itself, without remainder, into Christianity. Judaism, in its entirety, should have recognised and accepted Christ as the promised Messiah. That this manifestly did not happen is undisputed. Rather, Judaism, in its majority, continued on its historical way, declining the offer to join the Christian church. The upshot of Christianity's failure to absorb Judaism has been that Judaism has continued historically to be, as it were, a thorn in Christianity's flesh, a constant, uneasy reminder to Christianity that its claims may not be true, at least not in any self-evident or readily comprehensible sense.

Historically, Judaism has been Christianity's bad conscience, an unremitting, silent threat to the substance of Christianity's identity. Is it imaginable, then, that Christians could have been tempted to remove the thorn from their flesh, to stifle the fear and suspicion of possible error in their own self-understanding, by attempting to kill, and indeed wipe out all memory of, those whose continued existence was and remains an implicit question to the legitimacy of Christianity's claims? Is the need for identity so imperious in human beings that they will stop at nothing in order to satisfy it? Ironically, the so-called 'Jewish question' may, after all, really be the 'Christian question'.

CHRISTIANITY AND EUROPE[3]

At the present time, there are many voices, not least eminent clerical voices, being raised to remind us, as Europeans, of the danger of forgetting our Christian roots. This danger may have been less acute in a slightly earlier age. Forthright apologists for the church, like Hilaire Belloc, would have no hesitation in identifying 'The Faith', by which they meant Catholic Christianity, unproblematically with 'Europe'. And the expression 'Christian Europe' is indeed fairly standard in historical reference works: see, for instance, Hugh Trevor-Roper's *The Rise of Christian Europe* (1966). In fact it is quite a constant theme in western thought generally, since the German Romantics popularised it in such works as Novalis's *Christendom or Europe*. Yet notwithstanding this strong evidence for the Christian 'soul' of Europe – evidence powerfully supplemented by the virtually omnipresent, massive visibility of the influence of the Christian faith in the cities and landscapes of Europe, in cathedrals, monasteries, churches, chapels and shrines – when one begins to look a little more closely at the history of 'Europe', some at least of the 'roots of Europe' may not perhaps appear as specifically Christian at all, at any rate not specifically Christian in any simplistic sense. And perhaps more disquietingly, the specifically Christian 'root' of Europe is itself not without its ambiguities.

It is surely in no sense controversial to point out that one undeniable root of European culture owes nothing whatever, at least in its own origins, to Christianity. This is the root Europe inherited, like its very name, from ancient Greece. For Greece's principal contribution to the identity of what was to become Europe was well and truly formed before Christianity appeared on the scene. Indeed the Greek contribution to the future of Europe was formed in what would appear to have been total ignorance of the Jewish tradition from which Christianity eventually sprang. The same is true of the culture of ancient Rome, another essential ingredient of what later became 'Europe'. In fact, most of the major aspects of life in Europe, even today, as their very names suggest, are Greek or Roman in origin, not Christian, Jewish or biblical: economics, law, politics, tyranny, democracy, dictatorship, philosophy, literature, theatre, history, perhaps even the concept of 'religion' itself, to name but a few.

Apart, on the one hand, from Christianity proper, which emerged from Judaism, and, on the other hand, the cultures of ancient Greece and Rome, the other main root of Europe – again, in its origin at any rate, not a Christian root – was provided by the barbarian peoples who swept from east to west through the Roman Empire in late antiquity. In those chaotic days, Christianity was only a thin overlay, a veneer that never penetrated too deeply into the barbarian humus that made up and still makes up the body of Europe. Hence the permanent validity of such truisms as: 'Civilization is only ever skin-deep', or: 'Every generation is equidistant from barbarism.'

Christianity undoubtedly provided some of the glue helping to hold the vast edifice of early barbarian Europe together, and, equally, it was the vehicle transporting some elements of classical Graeco-Roman culture to the barbarians of Europe, as Islam, in its turn, was later to do. And it is also undoubtedly true to say that Christianity has, over the centuries, inspired great civilizing achievements in the areas of education, art, architecture, music and literature; some would even argue that modern science is unthinkable without the Christian – borrowed from the Jewish – doctrine of creation. Without this doctrine, would European thinkers ever have had the confidence to believe that the world was rationally comprehensible, even if inexhaustibly so, rather than a muddled, arbitrary minefield for the human mind? But in Christianity's name too, wars, slavery, crusades, inquisitions, pogroms and countless acts of indiscriminate brutality have been perpetrated. Indeed, the term 'slave' itself is a reminder of its origin during and after the age of Charlemagne, the 'Father of Europe', when, with the connivance of some European Christian rulers, the Vikings developed a lucrative slave trade, selling captured 'Slavs' to Muslim or Byzantine buyers.

In what is now called Central and South America, 'in the sixteenth century, in the name of the church, around eighty million Indios were annihilated. Tzvetan Todorov[4] writes: "The sixteenth century was to witness the greatest genocide in human history."'[5] This genocide was presided over by fervently Christian European nations. One final, dismaying reminder of the historical ambiguity of the term 'Christian' is the designation in Japan of the nuclear explosions that annihilated Hiroshima and Nagasaki in 1945 as 'the Christian bomb'. To date, only the 'Christian' West, in the 'person' of the United States of America, Europe's 'Wild West' (Gore Vidal), has in fact deployed nuclear weapons in situations of conflict.

The question might then be asked whether, in the course of its history, Christianity has done more harm than good. This question loses none of its poignancy or power to embarrass, even if it is pointed out that the calculus needed to accurately weigh up the pros and cons of Christianity's influence will presumably never be agreed upon.

Might it then perhaps be worth asking whether it could be a liability, rather than an asset, to have a religion as so substantial and so unambiguous a part of one's roots? Would it not be safer for religion to be distanced somewhat from the cultural process we call 'history'? Might Judaism's role in European history not offer a better ideal to aim at than the traditional role Christianity has played in the West? Judaism has acted as a moral and civilizing leaven in Europe, without being thoroughly absorbed by it, indeed being often rejected by Europe. So, might modern Europe's rejection of Christianity, if it is a rejection, not be a blessing in disguise, for both Christianity – and Europe?

Such considerations, however, could at best only offer pragmatic reasons for soft-pedalling Christianity's relationship with Europe. More theologically relevant, surely, is the belief that Christianity speaks of a 'kingdom' that is 'not of this world', not even of 'Europe'.

CHRISTIANITY AND THE ENLIGHTENMENT[6]

It could be argued that the European Enlightenment of the seventeenth and eighteenth centuries is not merely a product of the Christian tradition, but is itself in a quite specific sense reminiscent of the original emergence of Christianity in the world of late antiquity. Just as Christianity, as a cultural entity, grew out of Judaism (a Judaism that had for some three centuries of course been exposed to various levels of contact with Hellenistic civilization), so, *mutatis mutandis*, the Enlightenment grew out of the European Christian tradition. Early Christianity had been an uneasy, even potentially volatile, synthesis of Jewish and Hellenistic components. And in time, this synthesis was to become the 'soul' of the initially ramshackle political entity that arose from the corpse of the western Roman Empire in the wake of the barbarian invasions. Just how volatile the Christian tradition could be, the Enlightenment eventually revealed.

What is common, however, to the Enlightenment and Christianity is the fact that, for those involved in both movements, once the 'light' had dawned, there was no going back to a previous age or a more traditional world view. The only way to proceed was to go forward. Though, as we know from Paul, a return to Judaism remained a temptation, early Christians, on the whole, did not feel they could go back to the Judaism of their own past. Likewise, for the participants in the Enlightenment, there was no going back to a 'pre-critical' world.

Two further similarities are worth noting. First, neither movement wished to make, or did in fact make, a total, revolutionary break with its past (witness the fact that the early church did not reject the Hebrew scriptures, nor did the Enlightenment abandon the notion of 'the uniqueness and universality of truth'[7]). Second, the most committed participants in the new movements had to face the suspicion and often open hostility of members of the communities they sprang from (witness the persecution of the early Christians by certain elements in traditional Judaism, and the resistance to Enlightenment ideas by both church and state in the West down to quite recent times).

But perhaps for Christianity the most interesting conclusion to draw from the parallel invoked is the suspicion that, just as the emergence of Christianity did not mean the end of Judaism, the emergence of the Enlightenment, does not have to mean the end of Christianity. Rather, what the history of all three movements does appear to suggest is that, while 'truth' keeps on the move, thereby keeping us on our intellectual toes, the communities in which ultimate and abidingly resistant elements of the human condition were originally identified and articulated have continued to survive. What course the Christian church should now try to plot so as to incorporate the demands of critical thinking less timorously than heretofore within its own sense of being the embodiment of a religion connected to certain specific historical events, is a difficult question. It is one that theology may legitimately raise, but obviously cannot answer.

CATHOLICISM AND PROTESTANTISM[8]

At its inception in the early sixteenth century, Protestantism saw itself as a purified, 'reformed' expression of the Christian faith. In the eyes of the Protestant Reformers, Christianity had become corrupt in the hands of the Catholic church and needed to be restored to the alleged purity of its pristine beginnings.

Whatever about the accuracy of the Reformers' perception of early sixteenth-century Catholic Christianity, and whatever about the reservations one might have concerning the Reformed Churches' ability to deliver on their promise of a restored, purified Christianity, the Reformation does at least seem to have highlighted a fundamental, and perhaps irreconcilable split in the way Christianity can be construed.

Putting the matter in a potentially somewhat embarrassing nutshell, what the Reformation, more than earlier reform movements within western Christianity, appears to have succeeded in clarifying is that Catholicism is primarily a religion of 'externals', Protestantism a religion of 'internals'. Catholicism, with its stress on material creation, the external world, the sacraments (sacraments being traditionally regarded as the 'visible sign of invisible grace'), the body (whether glorified in baroque art or castigated for 'sins of the flesh'), or on physically attending mass on Sundays, is inextricably wedded to a vision of Christianity as a visible, tangible, palpable, in a word 'external' reality. Protestantism, on the other hand, with its stress on the individual's inner conviction, on his or her personal relationship with God, on the illumination of the Christian man or woman by the Holy Spirit, is inextricably wedded to a vision of Christianity as an essentially invisible, intangible, and, as far as human observation goes, imperceptible, in a word 'internal' reality.

In extreme cases, Catholicism can appear hypocritical to the point of being the very antithesis of Christianity, as the startling lines from a play by the Spanish dramatist Luis Vélez de Guevara insinuate: 'I can well be a bad Christian but a good Catholic.'[9] Protestantism, on the other hand, by playing off 'in Luther's words, "the wisdom of our flesh" and "the wisdom of the word of God"' (Walter Kaufmann), can create a strained, bogus spirituality, repudiated by Protestantism's most uncompromising critic, Friedrich Nietzsche, in the trenchant aphorism: 'Pure spirit is pure lie.'[10]

Could it be, then, that the Reformation was not about God at all – 'How can I find a gracious God?' (Luther's anguished question) – but about human beings, and the status of their material or bodily being? In yearning to abolish life's ambiguity, Protestantism was no doubt seeking to realise Christianity's most seductive promise. In resisting the temptation to be 'pure', Catholicism left itself open, as it must always do, to the charge of hypocrisy. But the silver lining of this particular cloud is that, by accepting that the body is a mask, not a mirror, of the soul ('persona' originally means 'mask'), Catholicism acknowledges human beings to be God's permanently ambiguous creatures, and God, the creator and redeemer, to be the only authentic interpreter of humanity's masks.

BEYOND THE TROUBLING NATURE OF CHRISTIAN HISTORY[11]

Today's gospel reading relays some of Jesus' words to his disciples at the Last Supper, before he was handed over to be executed. He begins by saying: 'Do not let your hearts be troubled. Trust in God still, and trust in me.' That advice is perhaps even more necessary for us today than it was for Jesus' first followers in their day. Their hearts could very understandably have been troubled because Jesus was giving them pretty clear hints that he was soon to leave them, soon to be condemned to death. So they would have been sad and worried, not just about the fate of Jesus, but also about the prospect of being abandoned, lost and confused, with Jesus dead and gone.

But, as I just said, maybe we should take Jesus' words even more to heart than the first disciples did. For it's one thing to be sad and troubled and anxious when you think that some disaster is about to strike you or your friends or your leader, as in the case of Jesus' first disciples, but since the time of Jesus, with the emergence and spread of the Christian church, a lot of disasters have been inflicted by Christians on other people. The Christian faith has not always been brought initially to other countries, as it was to Ireland, by purely peaceful means, but quite frequently with the Bible in one hand and a sword in the other, or rather often with a sword alone at the beginning, and only subsequently with the Bible.

The history of how western European nations colonised other parts of the world from the fifteen century onwards, bringing their Christian religion with them, is a mixed bag. While it includes the story of much self-sacrifice and heroic perseverance on the part of countless missionaries, it also tells the grim tale of how people were at times brutalised in the process of being converted to Christianity. In the twentieth century, some would argue that part of the reason for the destruction of many Jews in World War II was that Christian culture had encouraged suspicion and dislike of Jews down through the centuries. In our own country Christianity has been used for violent and destructive ends, and even the war in the Balkans at the end of the last century is seen by many as part of a centuries-old, still unresolved conflict between Latin (western) Christianity and the Orthodox Christian churches of the east. And this conflict has been complicated further by the inability of Christianity and Islam to find a way of living in peaceful co-existence.

All of these different examples can, of course, be argued about, or indeed even rejected as being damning for Christianity. But it must surely seem to any fair-minded observer that there is overwhelming evidence to suggest that Christian hands, after the last 2,000 years, are not all that lily-white or clean. And if some protest that the Christian conscience is clear, is that because it has rarely been used? Is it any wonder if many Christians are today troubled about all these matters?

If they are, if we are, worried, then we can get comfort from Jesus' words in today's gospel: 'Do not let your hearts be troubled. Trust in God still, and trust in me.' These words can bring us comfort, not in an easy sense of making us forget or deny the sinister side of ourselves or of our Christian past, but in the sense of reminding us of the main concerns of our faith. Our faith is a faith in Jesus as the divine saviour of the world, who by the sacrifice of his life on Calvary brought us to salvation, that is to say, gave us the possibility of getting to heaven. Christianity isn't about our own goodness or virtue, but about the goodness and the mercy of God who created and redeemed us and never abandons us, regardless of what horrors we may perpetrate or commit.

In the Easter season, we are reminded not just of Jesus' resurrection, but also of his appearances to his followers. These appearances tell us that Jesus didn't try to find new followers when he rose from the dead, but he returned to his old ones, even after and even though they had abandoned him to his fate on Calvary only a short time before.

So the good news, the gospel, of Jesus Christ is not just that God can forgive sin, and overcome evil and death, but that he still loves those who did and do continue to sin, and that he can overcome and deal with all the pain and sadness of our history and keep heaven always open for us as the final goal of our path through life.

Notes

Preface

1   Loosely translated: 'There is always love, always suffering, always death', a moving line from Suréna, the last tragedy, in his old age, by the seventeenth-century French playwright Pierre Corneille.

The Question of Creation

1   Friedrich Nietzsche, *Götzen-Dämmerung*, 'Die Vier Grossen Irrtümer' §8, in *Werke*, Vol. 2, ed. K. Schlechta (Munich: Hanser, 1960), p. 978.

2   First published, in a slightly different version, in *Irish Theological Quarterly* 66 (2001), p. 108, and subsequently in *The Word*, March 2006, Vol. 55, No. 3, p. 29.

3   A shorter version of this piece appeared first in *Irish Theological Quarterly* 71 (2006), pp. 348–9.

4   George Santayana, *Soliloquies in England and Later Soliloquies* (London: Constable & Company Ltd., 1922), p. 94.

5   First published in *Irish Theological Quarterly* 68 (2003), p. 34.

6   Frank Kermode, *The Genesis of Secrecy* (Cambridge, Mass.: Harvard University Press, 1979), p. 39.

7   First published in *Irish Theological Quarterly* 69 (2004), pp. 219–23.

8   Karl Barth, *Dogmatics in Outline*, tr. G.T. Thomson (London: SCM, 1949).

9   Ibid., p. 52.

10   Ibid., p. 54.

11   Citing Luther, Barth affirms 'that God, who does not need us, created heaven and earth and myself, [out] of "sheer fatherly kindness and compassion, apart from any merit or worthiness of mine"' (ibid., p. 54).

12   Ibid.

13   Ibid., p. 54f.

14   Ibid., p. 63f.

15   Quoted in J.M. and M.J. Cohen (eds), *The New Penguin Dictionary of Quotations* (Harmondsworth: Penguin, 1993), p. 321.

16   Theodor Adorno, *Minima Moralia* (Frankfurt a.M.: Suhrkamp, 1973), p. 333, quoted by Walter Kasper, *Jesus the Christ*, tr. V. Green (London/New York: Burns & Oates/Paulist Press, 1977), p. 56.

17   A homily for the second Sunday in Lent (Year C). Readings: Gen 15:5-12,

17-18; Phil 3:17-4, 1; Lk 9:28-36 (originally published under the title 'Transfiguration' in *The Furrow*, April 2007, pp. 231–33).

18 A phrase taken from the title of a sermon by Gerd Theissen (see Gerd Theissen, *The Sign Language of Faith*, tr. John Bowden (London: SCM, 1995), p. 147).

19 A homily for the fifth Sunday in Lent (Year B). Readings: Jer 31:31-34; Heb 5:7-9; Jn 12:20-33.

20 A homily for the 'World Day of the Sick'. First published under the title 'Why Does Christianity "Exalt" Sickness?' in *The Word*, February 2007, Vol. 56, No. 2, pp. 12–13.

21 Quoted in Leszek Kolakowski, *Religion*, (Oxford: OUP, 1982), p. 200.

22 Literally: 'Crush the infamous one (or thing)', usually taken to refer to the Christian church or the *ancien régime* in general, both of which were perceived as oppressive and intolerant by Voltaire and his fellow *philosophes*.

23 John McManners, *The French Revolution and the Church* (London: SPCK, 1969), p. 14.

24 John McManners, *Death and the Enlightenment* (Oxford: OUP, 1985), p. 123.

25 A late expression of this Enlightenment attitude can be found, for example, in Friedrich Nietzsche's *Anti-Christ*, §48, in his exegesis of Genesis 3.

26 Leszek Kolakowski, *Religion* (Oxford: OUP, 1982), p. 200.

27 Perhaps the notion of the 'fall of the angels' (see in the essay entitled, 'The Power of Angels') influenced the developing interpretation of the story of Adam and Eve in the early Christian era, so that humanity's story, too, came to be seen as involving a 'fall'. Or again, the early church's theology of the 'fall' may have been a concession to the plausibility of the Gnostic idea of creation as itself the 'fall', the 'fall into matter', as it were, matter being vulnerable to all-consuming time and its own entropy or in-built obsolescence.

28 *Faust*, Part One, 'Prologue in Heaven' ('For man must strive, and striving he must err', tr. Philip Wayne (Harmondsworth: Penguin, 1971), p. 4).

29 The last four paragraphs of this piece are a slightly reworked version of the conclusion of my article 'Original Sin: A Flawed Inheritance', *Irish Theological Quarterly* 65 (2000), pp. 3–12.

The Doctrine of God

1 A homily for the second Sunday in Advent (Year A). Readings: Is 11:1-10; Rom 15:4-9; Mt 3:1-12.

2 To quote a phrase by the Argentinian writer, Jorge Luis Borges.

3 A homily for the second Sunday in Advent (Year C). Readings: Bar 5:1-9; Phil 1:3-6, 8-11; Lk 3:1-6.

4 First published in *Irish Theological Quarterly* 64 (1999), p. 188.

5 For example, by Empedocles in the fifth century BC: 'God is a circle whose centre is everywhere and whose circumference is nowhere.' J.M. and M.J. Cohen, *The New Penguin Dictionary of Quotations* (Harmondsworth: Penguin, 1993), p. 159. At a later period, the German mystical theologian, Meister Eckhart, compared God 'to an infinite sphere the centre of which is everywhere and the circumference nowhere' (Maurice de Wulf, *History of Mediæval Philosophy*, Vol. II (London: Longmans, Green and Co., 1926), p. 129). [My note.]

6 Jorge Luis Borges, 'Pascal', in *Otras Inquisiciones* (Madrid: Alianza, 1976), pp. 99f.

7 *Otras Inquisiciones*, p. 16.

8 A homily for the eighth Sunday of Year C. Readings: Sir 27:4-7; 1 Cor 15:54-58; Lk 6:39-45. Some of the ideas in this homily are taken from Gerd Theissen, *Traces of Light* (London: SCM, 1996), and Leszek Kolakowski, op. cit.

9 A homily for the fourth (*Laetare*) Sunday in Lent (Year B). Readings: 2 Chron 36:14-16, 19-23; Eph 2:4-10; Jn 3:14-21 (originally published under the same title in *The Furrow*, May 1994, pp. 304–5).

10 Ludwig Wittgenstein, *Culture and Value*, ed. G.H. von Wright in collaboration with H. Nyman, tr. P. Winch (Oxford: Blackwell, 1980), p. 1e.

11 An expression of John Updike's; see John Updike, *Hugging the Shore: Essays and Criticism* (Harmondsworth: Penguin, 1985), p. 835.

12 Louis MacNeice, *Autumn Journal, A Poem*, xxiv; (London: Faber, 1943).

13 A homily for the twenty-first Sunday of Year C. Readings: Is 66:18-21; Heb 12:5-7, 11-13; Lk 13:22-30.

14 One might translate: 'The abuse of something doesn't rule out its proper application.'

15 *The Divine Comedy*, 3: Paradiso, Canto III, line 85.

16 A homily for Palm Sunday (Year C). Readings: Is 50:47; Phil 2:611; Lk 22:14-23:56 (originally published under the above title in *The Furrow*, May 1996, pp. 294–96).

17   A homily for Trinity Sunday (Year A). Readings: Ex 34:4-6, 8-9; 2 Cor 13:11-13; Jn 3:16-18.

18   A Homily for St Patrick's Day.

19   To the American theologian, Reinhold Niebuhr, is attributed the paradoxical saying that sin is not necessary, but it is inevitable.

20   A homily for the twenty-ninth Sunday of Year C. Readings: Ex 17:8-13; 2 Tim 3:14-4, 2; Lk 18:1-8.

21   'It is God alone who can never be sought in vain, even when he cannot be found' (quoted by Bernard McGinn in the introduction to Dennis Tamburello, OFM, *Ordinary Mysticism* (New York/Mahwah, N.J.: Paulist Press, 1996), p. x).

Grace and Redemption

1   This piece, which was a response to an article by Vincent Browne, first appeared in *Doctrine and Life*, Vol. 57, No. 5, May/June 2007, pp. 39–43, under the title, 'Christianity: a Blessing or a Scandal?' A shorter version, under the title, 'Christian faith tries to explain why we exist', was published in the 'Rite and Reason' column of *The Irish Times*, 21 August 2007, p. 14.

2   Quoted by Rudolf Wehrli, *Alter und Tod des Christentums bei Franz Overbeck* (Zurich: TVZ, 1977), p. 167.

3   Quoted by John Hick, *Evil and the God of Love* (London: Fontana, 1970), p. ix. This quip is used also, not unexpectedly, by Friedrich Nietzsche (*Ecce Homo*, 'Why I am so Clever,' §3, tr. R.J. Hollingdale (Harmondsworth: Penguin, 1980), p. 58).

4   Primo Levi, *The Drowned and the Saved*, tr. Raymond Rosenthal (London: Abacus, 1989), p. 117. (Jean Améry, the name taken in the 1930s by the Austrian Jewish intellectual Hans Mayer, also survived the Nazi death camps and also, like Primo Levi, eventually took his own life. The claim that Primo Levi's death was by suicide has, however, been called into question: see Diego Gambetta's article in the Summer 1999 issue of *Boston Review*.)

5   *Religion*, op. cit., p. 53.

6   Friedrich Nietzsche, *Thus Spoke Zarathustra*, Part 2, tr. R.J. Hollingdale (Harmondsworth: Penguin, 1986), p. 161

7   First published in *Irish Theological Quarterly* 67 (2002), p. 352.

8   First published under the title 'The Annunciation' in *Irish Theological*

Quarterly 68 (2003), pp. 160–62, and under the same title in *The Word*, March 2005, Vol. 54, No. 3, pp. 14–15.

9   See Gerd Theissen, *Die offene Tür: Biblische Variationen zu Predigttexten* (Munich: Kaiser Verlag, 1990), p. 67. For information on the mythical role of angels in Jewish culture prior to the emergence of Christianity, I am indebted to Gerd Theissen's reflections on the story of the Annunciation ('Die Verkündigung an Maria – ein Antimythos zur Geschichte von den lüsternen Engeln'), in ibid., pp. 66–9, from which many of the ideas in this piece derive.

10   See article 'Nephilim' by Ronald S. Hendel, in Bruce M. Metzger and Michael D. Coogan (eds), *The Oxford Companion to the Bible* (New York/Oxford: OUP, 1993), p. 556.

11   Theissen also points out that a passage like 1 Cor 11:10 ('… a woman ought to have a veil on her head, because of the angels') can be understood against the background of the meaning 'angels' had at the time of Christianity's emergence, except that unfortunately an element of 'demonising' (ibid., p. 68) of women has crept into the New Testament at this point. Women, Paul seems to be insinuating, could be seen as only too willing to cooperate with the 'angels', or in less mythical language, could be seen as taking too much advantage of the 'freedom' the new Hellenistic culture had imported into traditional Judaism, and so should be forced to hide their potentially seductive appeal. Theissen comments that the Jewish struggle with Hellenistic culture seems to have introduced a new anti-woman element into biblical thought – as can be seen, for instance, in the Pauline passage just cited – that was to have 'disastrous consequences' for the future (ibid., p. 68).

12   A homily for Christmas.

13   See the end of the poem, 'Ecco Homo', in David Gascoyne, *Poems, 1937–42* (London: Poetry, London/Nicholson & Watson, 1943), p. 7.

14   In *Road-side Dog* (New York: Farrar, Straus and Giroux, 1998), p. 19.

15   See *Beyond Good and Evil* §230, tr. R.J. Hollingdale, (Harmondsworth: Penguin, 1990), p. 162.

16   See, for example, his remarks in the second of the *Untimely Meditations*, tr. R.J. Hollingdale (Cambridge: CUP, 1983), p. 76: 'It requires a great deal of strength to be able to live and to forget the extent to which to live and to be unjust is one and the same thing.'

17   Cf. *Thus Spoke Zarathustra*, Part 2, tr. R.J. Hollingdale (Harmondsworth: Penguin, 1986), p. 161: 'To redeem the past and to transform every "It

was" into an "I wanted it thus!" – that alone do I call redemption!'

18   See Franz Overbeck, *Werke und Nachlaß*, Vol. 7/2, ed. Barbara von Reibnitz and Marianne Stauffacher-Schaub (Stuttgart/Weimar: Metzler, 1999), p. 214.

19   '[T]o dare to proclaim her love for disinterested thought, make[s] her a modern figure. If in her affirmation of the value of experience it is not illusory to see an instinctive reaction against the traditional thought of Spain, in her conception of knowledge – which she does not confuse with erudition, nor identify with religion – there is an implicit defence of intellectual conscience. Everything induces her to conceive of the world as a problem or as an enigma rather than as a place of salvation or perdition' (Octavio Paz, *El Laberinto de la Soledad* (Mexico: Fondo de Cultura Económica, 1982), p. 103).

20   Arthur Terry, *An Anthology of Spanish Poetry, 1500–1700 Part II 1580–1700* (Oxford: Pergamon Press, 1968), pp. 197–98.

21   From 'Two Songs from a Play', in William Butler Yeats, *Collected Poems* (London: MacMillan, 1977), p. 240.

22   Literally: 'An I-know-not-what that they [the creatures, who have caught a glimpse of God] keep stammering' (from the *Cántico Espiritual*).

23   First published in *Irish Theological Quarterly* 67 (2002), p. 152, and subsequently in *The Word*, June 2005, Vol. 54, No. 6, p. 29.

24   Martin Seymour-Smith, *The 100 Most Influential Books Ever Written: The History of Thought From Ancient Times to Today* (New York: Citadel Press, 2001), p. 12. The *tikkun* itself, Gershom Scholem defined as 'the restitution of cosmic harmony through the earthly medium of a mystically elevated Judaism' (quoted in Sander L. Gilman and Jack Zipes (eds), *Yale Companion to Jewish Writing and Thought in German Culture, 1096–1996* (New Haven and London: Yale University Press, 1997), p. 408). For an overview of the Kabbalah, see Gershom Scholem, *Kabbalah* (New York: Meridian/Penguin, 1978).

25   S.L. Gilman and J. Zipes (eds), op. cit., p. 720.

26   See Paul Celan, *Selected Poems*, tr. and intro. Michael Hamburger (Harmondsworth: Penguin, 1990), p. 29.

27   See G. Scholem, *Die jüdische Mystik in ihren Hauptströmungen* (Frankfurt a/M: Suhrkamp, 1980), Chapter 8, on the Messianism of the tragic figure, Sabbatai Zevi.

28   A homily for the third Sunday of Easter (Year B). Readings: Acts 3:13-15, 17-19; 1 Jn 2:1-5; Lk 24:35-48.

29   A homily for the sixth Sunday of Easter (Year B). Readings: Acts 10:25-26, 34-35, 44-48; 1 Jn 4:7-10; Jn 15:9-17.

30   A homily for the Solemnity of Christ the King (Year C). Readings: 2 Sam 5:1-3; Col 1:12-20; Lk 23:35-43. I should like to thank John Campbell for his editorial suggestions and advice on this piece.

The Doctrine of Christ

1   A homily for the Feast of Corpus Christi (Year C). Readings: Gen 14:18-20; 1 Cor 11:23-26; Lk 9:11-17.

2   'Out of timber so crooked as that from which man is made nothing entirely straight can be built' (Immanuel Kant, quoted by Isaiah Berlin as an epigraph to his book *The Crooked Timber of Humanity*, London: Fontana, 1991, p. v).

3   A homily for the Feast of the Assumption.

4   A homily for the third Sunday of Easter (Year A). Readings: Acts 2:14, 22-28; 1 Pet 1:17-21; Lk 24:13-35 (originally published under the title 'Talking to Strangers' in *The Furrow*, June 1997, pp. 363–5).

The Kingdom of Heaven

1   A homily for Thursday of the second week in Advent (Feast of St John of the Cross). Readings: Is 41:13-20; Mt 11:11-15.

2   In the dedication of the second edition of *How Christian is our Present-Day Theology?* (1903) to his former pupil, Carl Albrecht Bernoulli, Franz Overbeck had alluded playfully to Mt 11:12, intimating that, in one of his own publications, Bernoulli had seriously misinterpreted the first edition of Overbeck's work (1873). See Franz Overbeck, *How Christian is Our Present-day Theology?*, annotated translation with an introduction by Martin Henry; with a foreword by David Tracy (London: T & T Clark/Continuum, 2005), p. 4: 'If even the Kingdom of Heaven, according to the Gospels, must suffer being taken by force by men of violence, how on earth could this little book of mine dream of reacting with indignation, and nothing but indignation, at your former assault upon it!'

3   A homily for the sixth Sunday of Year C. Readings: Jer 17:5-8; 1 Cor 15:12, 16-20; Lk 6:17, 20-26.

4   A homily for the twenty-eighth Sunday of Year A. Readings: Is 25:6-10; Phil 4:12-14, 19-20; Mt 22:1-14.

5   A homily for the Feast of the Transfiguration of the Lord (Year B). Readings: Dan 7:9-10, 13-14; 2 Pet 1:16-19; Mk 9:2-10.

6   As Les Murray's short poem, 'The Knockdown Question', for example, implies: 'Why does God not spare the innocent?/The answer to that is not in/the same world as the question/so you would shrink from me/in terror if I could answer it' (from *Poems the Size of Photographs*, Sydney: Duffy & Snellgrove, 2002, p. 67).

7   A homily for the third (*Gaudete*) Sunday in Advent (Year A). Readings: Is 35:1-6, 10; Jas 5:7-10; Mt 11:2-11 (originally published under the title 'Joy in Hope' in *The Furrow*, September 1999, pp. 482–4).

8   An aphorism of the Polish writer Stanislaw Jerzy Lec.

Between Heaven and Earth

1   A homily for the second Sunday of Year C. Readings: Is 62:1-5; Cor 12:4-11; Jn 2:1-12.

2   A slightly expanded version of a homily preached on Sunday, 5 June 2005 in the Sacred Heart church, Belfast, at the close of the Forty Hours' Adoration, marking the hundredth anniversary of the foundation of the Sacred Heart parish. Readings for the Feast of the Sacred Heart (Year B): Hos 11:1, 3-4, 8-9; Eph 3:8-12, 14-19; Jn 19:31-37.

3   Miguel de Unamuno, *La Agonía del Cristianismo* (Madrid: Espasa-Calpe, 1966), p. 114: 'El culto al Sagrado Corazón de Jesús, la *hierocardiocracia*, es el sepulcro de la religión cristiana.'

4   A slightly revised version of a homily for the fifth Sunday of Year C. Readings: Is 6:1-8; 1 Cor 15:1-11; Lk 5:1-11 (originally published under the title 'What are you fishing for?' in *The Furrow*, June 1998, pp. 350–2).

5   *Human, All Too Human*, Vol. 1, §87 (a sardonic comment on Lk 18:14).

6   A phrase from the German poet Heinrich Heine (see his poem 'Die Götter Griechenlands' ['The Gods of Greece']).

7   Kolakowski, op. cit., p. 53.

8   And yet, in another mood, Goethe could speak of Christianity as revealing to humanity, 'the divine depth of suffering' ('*die göttliche Tiefe des Leidens*': in *Wilhelm Meisters Wanderjahre*, quoted in Karl Löwith, *Von Hegel zu Nietzsche* (Hamburg: Meiner, 1978), p. 37).

9   The complexities of Nietzsche's relationship to Christianity cannot be developed here. See my *On not understanding God* (Dublin: Columba, 1997), Chapter 9 ('The Nietzsche Factor').

10   A homily for the twelfth Sunday of Year C. Readings: Zech 12:10-11; Gal 3:26-29; Lk 9:18-24.

11   A homily for the fifth Sunday in Lent (Year C). Readings: Is 43:16-21; Phil 3:8-14; Jn 8:1-11.

12   A homily for the seventh Sunday of Year C. Readings: 1 Sam 26:2, 7-9, 12-13, 22-23; 1 Kgs 15:45-49; Lk 6:27-38.

Religion and Morality

1   A homily for the eleventh Sunday of Year C. Readings: 2 Sam 12:7-10, 13; Gal 2:16, 19-21; Lk 7:36-8:3.

2   The so-called 'antinomian' (literally: anti-law) tendency in Christianity surfaced as early as St Paul's own day, although the term itself was apparently first used by Martin Luther.

3   A homily for the third Sunday in Lent (Year C). Readings: Ex 3:1-8, 13-15; 1 Cor 10:1-6, 10-12; Lk 13:1-9.

4   A homily for the third Sunday in Lent (Year A). Readings: Ex 17:3-7; Rom 5:1-2, 5-8; Jn 4:5-42.

5   A homily for the fourth Sunday of Year C. Readings: Jer 1:4-5, 17-19; 1 Cor 12:1-13; Lk 4:21-30.

6   I am here adapting a famous formulation by La Rochefoucauld, when he wrote that 'hypocrisy is the homage vice pays to virtue'.

Church Matters

1   A homily for the first Sunday in Lent (Year B). Readings: Gen 9:8-15; 1 Pet 3:18-22; Mk 1:12-15.

2   'Men never do evil so completely and cheerfully as when they do it from religious conviction': a saying of the French seventeenth-century religious apologist Pascal, as cited in David Tracy, *Plurality and Ambiguity* (London: SCM, 1988), p. 86, quoting from Richard John Neuhaus, *The Naked Public Square: Religion and Democracy in America* (Grand Rapids, MI: Eerdmans, 1984), p. 8.

3   A homily for Pentecost. Readings: Acts 2:1-11; 1 Cor 12:3-7, 12-13; Jn 20:19-23.

4   Stanislaw Jerzy Lec, *Sämtliche Unfrisierte Gedanken* (Zürich: Sanssouci Verlag, 1999), p. 15 ('*Schade, dass man ins Paradies mit einem Leichenwagen fährt*').

5   I am exploiting here an idea found in the writings of the late James Barr,

e.g. in the article 'Historical Reading and the Theological Interpretation of Scripture,' in: J. Barr, *Explorations in Theology 7* (London: SCM, 1980), pp. 34–5.

6   A homily for Mission Sunday. Readings: Is 53:10-11; Acts 10:34, 37-43; Jn 3:16-18 (originally published under the title 'Mission Sunday', in *The Furrow*, December 2000, pp. 669–72).

7   For the reference to Las Casas, I am indebted to Jorge Luis Borges, *A Universal History of Infamy*, tr. Norman Thomas di Giovanni (Harmondsworth: Penguin, 1975), p. 19.

8   Friedrich Nietzsche, *The Anti-Christ*, tr. R.J. Hollingdale (Harmondsworth: Penguin, 1990), p. 161.

Christianity and Power

1   A homily for the first Sunday in Lent (Year C). Readings: Deut 26:4-10; Rom 10:8-13; Lk 4:1-13.

2   A homily for the twenty-ninth Sunday of Year A. Readings: Is 45:1, 4-6; 1 Thess 1:1-5b; Mt 22:15-21. Most of the ideas in this homily are taken from a sermon on Mt 22:15-22 by Petra von Gemünden, in Gerd Theissen, *The Sign Language of Faith: Opportunities for Preaching Today*, tr. John Bowden (London: SCM, 1995), p. 143ff.

3   Taken from the title of the sermon on Mt 22:15-22 by Petra von Gemünden, ibid.

4   A homily for the Solemnity of Christ the King (Year B). Readings: Dan 7:13-14; Rev 1:5-8; Jn 18:33-37.

Death and Eternal Life

1   First published in *Irish Theological Quarterly*, 66 (2001), p. 390, and subsequently in *The Word*, January 2005, Vol. 54, No. 1, p. 18.

2   Gore Vidal, *Julian* (London: Abacus, 1993), p. 403.

3   Harold Bloom, *How to Read and Why* (New York: Scribner, 2000), p. 186.

4   '*Das Leben borgt seinen höchsten Reiz vom Tode; es ist nur schön, weil es vergänglich ist,*' quoted from Hebbel's *Tagebücher*, in Friedemann Spicker (ed.), *Aphorismen der Weltliteratur* (Stuttgart: Reclam, 1999), p. 98. This is possibly an echo of a couplet by Goethe: '*Warum bin ich vergänglich, o Zeus? So fragte die Schönheit/Macht ich doch, sagte der Gott, nur das Vergängliche schön*' ('Beauty asked: "Why must I perish, oh Zeus?" "Why, I gave beauty", answered the god, "only to perishable

things"', tr. David Luke, *Goethe* (Harmondsworth: Penguin, 1972), p. 129).

5   A homily for the first Sunday in Advent (Year A). Readings: Is 2:1-5; Rom 13:11-14; Mt 24:37-44 (originally published under the title 'Meeting God', in *The Furrow*, May 2005, pp. 302–4).

6   First published in *Irish Theological Quarterly* 68 (2003), 324, and under the title 'Language and Nothing' in *The Word*, February 2005, Vol. 54, No. 2, p. 18.

7   A homily given on the occasion of a mass for the deceased benefactors of St Patrick's College, Maynooth, in the autumn of 1992. Readings: Job 19:23-27; Rom 8:31-35, 37-39; Mt 11:25-30. A version of this homily was published, under the above title, in *The Furrow*, December 1992, pp. 678–80, and subsequently as the 'Postlude' to my *On not understanding God* (Dublin: Columba, 1997).

8   Hugo Rahner, *Man At Play* (New York: Herder and Herder, 1972), pp. 84–86.

9   A homily for the nineteenth Sunday of Year C. Readings: Wis 18:6-9; Heb 11:1-2, 8-19; Lk 3:32-48.

10   A homily for the Feast of the Ascension (Year B). Readings: Acts 1:1-11; Eph 1:17-23; Mk 16:15-20.

11   See Friedrich Nietzsche, *Human, All Too Human*, tr. R.J. Hollingdale (Cambridge, CUP, 1986), p. 299: '*Eternal liveliness* ... is what counts: what do "eternal life", or life at all, matter to us!' Elsewhere, in a famous poem, Nietzsche in fact uses the term 'eternity' itself with a positive resonance in order to express his desire that joy should never end: '"woe says: Fade! Go!/But all joy wants eternity,/Wants deep, deep, deep eternity!"' (*Thus Spoke Zarathustra*, tr. R.J. Hollingdale (Harmondsworth: Penguin, 1986) p. 333.)

12   See http://en.wikipedia.org/wiki/Walter_Kaufmann_(philosopher).

13   A homily for the Feast of the Assumption.

Aspects of the History of Christianity

1   First published in *Irish Theological Quarterly* 70 (2005), p. 366.

2   First published in *Irish Theological Quarterly* 70 (2005), p. 362.

3   First published in this version in *The Furrow*, January 2007, p. 56–8. A shorter version was published previously in *Irish Theological Quarterly*, 70 (2005), p. 132.

4   A Bulgarian intellectual (born 1939), who now lives in France.

5   Norbert Greinacher, in J. Moltmann (ed.), *How I Have Changed. Reflections on Thirty Years of Theology* (London: SCM, 1997), p. 51.

6   First published in *Irish Theological Quarterly* 69 (2004), p. 188.

7   Ernest Gellner, *Postmodernism, Reason and Religion* (London/New York: Routledge, 1992), p. 58. Gellner characterises the faith of the Enlightenment thus: 'Rationalism was the continuation of exclusive monotheism by other means' (ibid.).

8   First published in *Irish Theological Quarterly* 70 (2005), p. 262.

9   Quoted by Gerald Brenan in *The Literature of the Spanish People* (Harmondsworth: Penguin, 1963), p. 412.

10   *The Antichrist*, §8, tr. R.J. Hollingdale.

11   A homily for the fifth Sunday of Easter (Year A). Readings: Acts 6:1-7; 1 Pet 2:4-9; Jn 14:1-12.

Index of Homilies

This index is a rough guide, by liturgical season and yearly cycle (A/B/C) for the most part, to where the homilies scattered throughout this book are located.

Index of Names